INSIGHT

INSIGHT

The Series

A Hollywood Priest's Groundbreaking Contribution to Television History

**by
Mark A. Villano**

BearManor Media
2022

INSIGHT

© 2022 *Mark A. Villano*

All rights reserved.

No portion of this publication may be reproduced, stored, and/or copied electronically (except for academic use as a source), nor transmitted in any form or by any means without the prior written permission of the publisher and/or author.

Published in the United States of America by:

BearManor Media

4700 Millenia Blvd.
Suite 175 PMB 90497
Orlando, FL 32839

bearmanormedia.com

Printed in the United States.

Typesetting and layout by BearManor Media

ISBN—978-1-62933-902-3

Contents

Acknowledgements	vii
Foreword	ix
I. The Impact of *Insight*	1
II. The Episodes	5
III. After *Insight*	179
IV. Epilogue: The Spirituality of the "Hollywood Priest"	181
Appendix: The Writers and Directors	188
Bibliography/Notes	200
Index	203

Acknowledgements

Compiling the list of episodes, relevant data, and production photos for the twenty-three-year history of *Insight* was only possible because of the support of the staff at Paulist Productions. I'm grateful to Michael Sullivan, President at Paulist Productions, Fr. Tom Gibbons, C.S.P., Vice President, and David Moore, Director of Development and Production. All pictures are from the Paulist Productions collection, and most of the quotes presented in the episode section are from interviews conducted by Fr. Tom Gibbons or the author. Others are excerpted from Television Academy Foundation interviews.

Completion of the filmography could not have proceeded without the assistance of Mark Quigley, the John H. Mitchell Television Curator at the UCLA Film and Television Archive. His interest in preserving *Insight* has been vital in making the series accessible to future viewers and researchers. The Archive's online catalogue was a significant research resource for this project. I'm happy that Pierre Patrick and Ben Ohmart of Bear Manor Media agreed that *Insight* "deserves a book."

The ongoing mission of Paulist Productions is the true legacy of Fr. Ellwood ("Bud") Kieser, C.S.P., who founded the company in 1960, and who died on December 16, 2000, at the age of 71. His many co-workers over the years were a foundational support for his vision. These include longtime collaborators like Joseph Connelly, Jack Shea, Jane Murray, John Furia, John Meredyth Lucas, Lan O'Kun, Terry Sweeney, Judy Greening, and Mike Rhodes. I especially want to recognize Fr. Bud's Paulist brothers who joined him in this work, before and after his death: Jack Mulhall, C.S.P., Tom Hollahan, C.S.P., Gregory Apparcel, C.S.P., Frank Desiderio, C.S.P., Eric Andrews, C.S.P., Thomas Gibbons, C.S.P.

Foreword

If St. Clare of Assisi is the patron saint of television, Fr. Ellwood Kieser is the patron saint of "4 AM television"—the lonely, mostly pre-24-hour cable, predawn broadcast landscape, once populated by a captive audience of barflies, insomniacs, and the dispossessed and distressed. Such non-Nielsen, way-past primetime viewers were Fr. Kieser's cathode-ray tube parishioners, and I became one of them by a chance flip of the TV dial.

Fr. Kieser, a.k.a., the "Hollywood Priest," launched his long-running syndicated religious series *Insight* in 1960, the same year CBS' acclaimed anthology drama *Playhouse 90* ceased production, symbolically marking the end of the golden age of television. Over the following decades, however, Fr. Kieser would keep the once-venerated television anthology genre alive with *Insight*—hosting, producing, and occasionally writing his outré humanist series that had more in common with *The Twilight Zone* than a Sunday morning TV sermon.

Unfortunately, after several brief but successful forays into primetime, by the latter half of the 1970s and onward, Fr. Kieser's experimentally minded, low-budget *Insight* series was mainly relegated to the wee hours of the Sunday morning programming ghetto, alongside other broadcast ephemera nearing extinction, such as test patterns and national anthem sign-offs. Within this twilight television netherworld, my involvement with the *Insight* series began.

In the winter of 1994, jolted awake at an ungodly hour by an unnerving aftershock to California's severe Northridge earthquake, I turned to my television for the reassuring local omniscience of Channel 7's Eyewitness News. Surprisingly, I found instead an eerie, obviously vintage teledrama featuring familiar actor Brian

Keith hulking around a sparsely decorated set, devastated that his estranged son's bad LSD trip may have contributed to a tragic murder. The series was *Insight*. The episode, "The Sandalmaker" (1968), was complex in its social issue messaging and overtly grim tone—its 4 AM broadcast slot unsettling yet somehow appropriate given the story's gravitas.

Fast forward: working as a moving image archivist nearly a decade after my chance encounter with the hauntingly compelling "Sandalmaker," professional curiosity (compounded by an absence of detailed reference resources) prompted me to cold-call Paulist Productions, the company behind *Insight*, to inquire as to the fate of their ambitious series, which by 2003 had been driven from the airwaves altogether by all-night infomercials. To my surprise, the kind staff at Paulist headquarters indicated that *Insight* holdings did survive, though entombed in the unlikeliest of places—the dank recesses of film director Roland West's infamous, historic oceanfront property on the Pacific Coast Highway. On that fateful site in 1935, under suspicious circumstances, West's lover and business partner, screen star Thelma Todd (a.k.a. "Hot Toddy," featured with the Marx Brothers in *Monkey Business* and *Horse Feathers*) was found in the garage, slumped over the steering wheel of her convertible, dead at age thirty.

The storied Pacific Palisades, California building with a dark past ultimately found its way to the Paulists via West's second wife, actress Lola Lane of the singing Lane Sisters (and costar alongside Bette Davis in 1937's *Marked Woman*). After remarrying and converting to Catholicism, Lane and her husband Robert Hanlon became taken with Fr. Kieser. They allowed the priest to utilize the ground floor for production offices, eventually selling the entire property to the Paulists at a fraction of market cost. The irony of the site of Todd's scandalous death as the setting for a religious TV production company was not lost on the notoriously resourceful Fr. Kieser, who only half-jokingly told a reporter that the Paulists "exorcised the place before we moved in."

After decades in television production, the Paulists adapted several sections of the humid underbelly of Todd's former haunt for storage of their master and circulation film and tape elements. Through these dark, damp, expansive catacombs, a Paulist Productions staff member led UCLA's Television Archivist Dan Einstein and me to the Holy Grail—hundreds of kinescopes and videoreels of *Insight*. Our first assessment of the find brought both relief and concern. On the positive side, Paulist staff and volunteers had done an admirable job of shelving and organizing many of the legacy holdings—row after row of rusty 16mm cans and weathered but sturdy 1- and 2-inch videoreel cases. More worrisome was the lack of suitability of the physical space—dusty, balmy, with exposed pipes snaking through the basement area and a saggy, water-stained ceiling overhead. Only a small home-use dehumidifier chugged away in a corner for environmental control. Thankfully, our initial inspection of the films and magnetic media revealed no signs of mold or other severe condition issues.

As befits a religious nonprofit, these improvised vault spaces were the only fiscal option available to the Paulists for their collection's substantial storage needs. Father Frank Desiderio, successor to the late Fr. Kieser and then president of Paulist Productions, welcomed UCLA's intervention.

With Fr. Desiderio's blessing, formal deposit terms were agreed upon, which allowed UCLA Film & Television Archive to become the long-term custodian of Paulist Productions' physical *Insight* holdings. As the series was prolifically syndicated for decades and actively marketed on 16mm to schools and churches via catalog sales, the Paulists held redundant copies of many episodes across multiple physical formats. Our first task was to sort through these holdings to locate 2-inch videoreel masters where extant, or best available versions on 1-inch videoreels and 16mm prints where they were not. After numerous visits to the Paulist offices, UCLA accessioned over 450 items, representing nearly the entire run of the *Insight* series. Much of our initial preservation work, concentrated on migrating 2-inch video masters of *Insight*, was conducted at the former CBS Videotape Annex, part of CBS Television City in Hollywood, where Fr. Kieser originally produced and taped the series.

Now, close to three decades after my fortuitous 4 AM encounter with *Insight*, as an archivist and curator, it has been my continued privilege to preserve the series' legacy and present Fr. Kieser's work to new audiences. UCLA's screenings of preserved episodes of *Insight* at academic conferences and cinematheques in New York, Chicago, and Los Angeles have been met by receptive audiences—captivated by the otherworldliness of Fr. Kieser's creation and the improbable story of how (and where) it survived to be archived.

In the pages that follow, Father Mark Villano offers a long-overdue reference companion to *Insight* that illuminates, on a per-episode level, the full scope and scale of Fr. Kieser's lasting contribution to the medium of television and the genre of anthology drama. Episode entries detail the stunning list of talent enlisted in the production of the series, from Ivan Dixon to Ida Lupino, and the heavy topics tackled, which included fear of death, greed, nuclear war, suicide, among others. Perfect reading for 4 AM.

Mark Quigley
Television Curator
UCLA Film & Television Archive
Portions of this foreword originally appeared in
The Moving Image
Volume 9, Number 1, Spring 2009
University of Minnesota Press

- 1 -
The Impact of *Insight*

The anthology television series *Insight*, which ran for twenty-three seasons from 1960 to 1983, is one of the longest running weekly syndicated shows in television history. It won several Emmys as well as other awards. It attracted the talents of such premier actors as Jane Wyman, Raymond Massey, Jack Klugman, Vera Miles, Walter Matthau, Martin Sheen, Ed Asner, Carol Burnett, Brian Keith, Ricardo Montalban, Cicely Tyson, Gene Hackman, Lou Gossett, Jr., Bob Newhart, Celeste Holm, Beau and Jeff Bridges, and Melinda Dillon. It provided a vehicle for writers like Michael Crichton, Rod Serling, Gilbert Ralston, Jack Hanrahan, William Peter Blatty, James Moser, Howard Fast, Carol Sobiesky, Edmund H. North, John Sacret Young, and John McGreevy to deal with profound human questions in an entertaining way. Directors like Arthur Hiller, Ted Post, Norman Lloyd, Delbert Mann, Robert Butler, Ralph Senensky, Buzz Kulik, and Hal Cooper added their creative weight to the shows.

The series was like an experimental theatre. It fostered an atmosphere of creative freedom. It utilized comedy, drama, and fantasy. It sought to bring a moral seriousness to the television landscape of its day. Yet, the series is hardly known today. It was aired at odd times (and always without commercials). It was considered filler for local stations seeking FCC "public interest credits" (tax rebates) for providing nonprofit community service programming, a system that ended with the deregulation of the early 1980s.

Insight, however, could not fail to garner recognition for its willingness to tackle modern anxieties and controversial topics head on. As such it was considered an outstanding example of religious programming, maintaining both its social relevance and its spiritual bearings.

So, how did this amazing story begin?

In 1956, Fr. Ellwood Kieser, who went by the name "Bud," arrived in Los Angeles to serve at St. Paul the Apostle Church. The parish was administered by his community, the Paulist Fathers, a Catholic order of priests attuned to dialogue with secular culture. One of his duties was to teach an "Inquiry Class," a venue for people who wanted to learn more about Christianity and the Catholic faith. Impressed by the young priest's erudition and communication style, some parishioners, who happened to be television producers, encouraged him to explore media as a way to increase his audience. The CBS affiliate in L.A., KNXT, agreed to give him 13 half hour time slots on Sunday afternoons. *Insight* was born.

The first season, begun in 1960, consisted of little more than the priest's lectures, albeit interspersed at times with dramatic readings. The second season moved to a dramatic format and the show was offered to stations around the country for free. *Insight* became a national program that got noticed by some of Hollywood's best working writers, directors, and actors. They saw how Fr. Kieser respected talent and creativity, and viewed his program as an opportunity to work on projects that tried to do something different from the usual commercial fare. Many even donated their time and skill.

Eventually, the Paulists asked Fr. Bud to engage his television work full-time. Like all filmmaking, television is a collaborative art form, and the creative people Fr. Bud brought together to produce *Insight* became part of his new "parish." He became pastorally involved in their lives, whether they were Christian or Jewish, believers or unbelievers. Fr. Bud wanted them to feel accepted and welcomed into the artistic process. As a result, Paulist Productions, the company he founded to produce *Insight*, became a hard-working, loving community.

This is not to say that frustrations and crises did not surface. Conflicts are inevitable in the context of intense group dynamics of any kind, let alone those that combine the creative, financial, and personal investments of show business. Fr. Kieser was continually frustrated with the time slots offered to *Insight*, while others at times questioned what they considered his overbearing leadership style. Mission trips and retreats helped him to stay centered and keep from burning out.

Each year, Fr. Bud wondered if he would come up with enough new ideas to keep the series fresh. Year after year, though, new seasons of *Insight* were produced. In his autobiography, *Hollywood Priest*, Fr. Kieser described his process of sitting down with a writer and sharing ideas he had come up with for future episodes.[1] Sometimes one idea would spark something in the writer's subconscious. Story conferences would follow that took on the character of a confessional. Producer and writer would shed their defenses and talk with one another in a deeply honest way. With Fr. Bud's stimulation and guidance, the writer's imagination then took over.

Over the course of many seasons, Fr. Kieser saw the shows falling into three general categories: "God shows," focused on the divine-human connection; "love shows," focused on the human relationship with self or others; and "justice shows," dealing with societal problems. Interestingly, he found the comedic approach especially well-suited for the God shows. He wrote: "The interfacing of the divine and human is so charged with incongruity, so full of surprises, and so prone to vulnerability that it quite naturally lends itself to comedy. God can be funny."[2]

After much effort, some stations did start airing *Insight* "holiday specials" in prime time. However, by the early 1980s, changes in FCC rules were having their effect. Fewer and fewer stations were interested in hosting programming from mainline religious groups for free when those time slots could be sold to televangelists or advertiser-sponsored programs. The decision was made to cease production of *Insight*.

Fr. Bud had poured twenty-three years of his life into a series that had made a significant contribution to values-based television. The UCLA Film and Television Archives acquired the tapes of all the *Insight* shows (231 extant episodes), as well as other Paulist television productions from that period, to put them in protective storage. The archivists thought they were a valuable artifact of a unique chapter in television history. Since then, Paulist Productions has set up a YouTube channel to access the series so that a new generation of viewers can find *Insight*.[3]

The ending of the series was not a finale for Fr. Bud's involvement in the entertainment industry. As we shall see, Paulist Productions went on to produce mainstream television movies and documentaries, as well as feature films. It continues to carry on Fr. Ellwood Kieser's vision. "Jesus was a storyteller," Fr. Bud said. "He told stories in order to challenge people and illumine the meaning of their lives and motivate them to love. I would like to think I make movies for the same purpose."[4]

In exploring the chronological history of *Insight* in the section that follows, one may be impressed with how, in admittedly dated material, perennial human questions and hopes are addressed in astute and entertaining ways. Equally impressive is how a generation of creative artists and their supporters pulled together to bring it about.

- II -

INSIGHT

1960-1983

The Episodes

This section provides a year-by-year run down of each *Insight* episode. The key creators (writer, director, actors) are listed as well as short synopses. Photos and some written material, including interviews with actors and collaborators, and passages from scripts, are from the Paulist Productions collection unless otherwise cited. Excerpts of Fr. Kieser's commentary from particular episodes are edited for readability.

1960-61

Fr. Kieser taught a popular class at his parish to people who were interested in learning more about the Catholic faith. *Insight* began as way for him to widen his audience. The first season of the show presented lectures on various religious topics, as the episode titles indicate.

Few of these earliest episodes have survived, and incomplete information is available for them. Those that do survive show an appreciation for the visual needs of a television production. As Fr. Kieser lectured, he moved around a contemporary office setting with bookshelves and maps on the wall, while cutting to slides depicting historical scenes or art works. Eventually, actors would participate in dramatic readings or vignettes.

The opening credits of the first shows included the following introduction: "*Insight*: A series of programs devoted to the meaning and mystery of Christendom's oldest faith, the teachings and traditions of the Catholic Church. Brought to you each week by America's missionaries to main street, the Paulist Fathers."

Joseph Connelly, an accomplished television writer and producer, known for creating the popular show *Leave It to Beaver*, was the first producer to assist Fr. Kieser on *Insight*.

Episode numbers are those used by Paulist Productions and show some gaps and inconsistencies.

#101 A Tale of Two Testaments

Producer: Joseph Connelly; Director: Mike Cozzi; Writer and Host: Ellwood Kieser

The first episode of *Insight* was announced by TV Guide on October 16, 1960, with the logline: "Paulist Father Ellwood Kieser begins this new religious series with a look at the Hebrew people." The show examines the Old Testament through a Christian lens and makes a case against anti-Semitism.

Fr. Ellwood Kieser, C.S.P.

From Fr. Kieser's teaching in "A Tale of Two Testaments"

The God of the Israelites is a God of mercy and love and forgiveness. He is a God of justice. And so, it is impossible that he would create mankind and predestine one percent for salvation and forget all about the other ninety-nine percent. What is the logical alternative? There is only one. God loves all his creatures. He wills the salvation and eternal happiness of every single one of his rational creatures. God selected the Jewish people, and he lavished his love upon them that through them, he might provide spiritual enrichment for the entire human race...

#102 **Who is Christ?** *(Lost episode)*

#103 **Secret Life of God** *(Lost episode)*

#104 A Reason to Live, and a Reason to Die

Producer: Joseph Connelly; Director: Mike Cozzi; Writer and Host: Ellwood Kieser

Choreographer: David Lichine

Fr. Kieser lectures on the human quest for meaning as a movement beyond egoism and hedonism to an openness to God and divine revelation. Dancers provide dramatic accents to the lecture.

> Fr. Kieser's prologue to "A Reason to Live, and a Reason to Die"
>
> In a far corner of the universe, there's a very remarkable planet. How long it's been there is uncertain. But we are certain it does support human life. Many of its inhabitants are as remarkable as the race itself. They've been walking around on it for some time now, and yet they seem to know very little about it. In fact, they seem to know very little about themselves. The planet, of course, is earth. The inhabitants, the human race...

#105 Conversation with Christ *(Lost episode)*

#106 Happiness *(Lost episode)*

#107 Where Are We Going? *(Lost episode)*

#108 The Mission of the Apostles *(Lost episode)*

#109 What Is the Church? *(Lost episode)*

#110 Christian Marriage

Producer: Joseph Connelly; Director: Jim Johnson; Writer: Ellwood Kieser.

Fr. Kieser lectures on the sacrament of marriage and its impact on the Christian way of life. He reflects on marriage as a "school of love" that unites a man and woman for the sake of their physical and emotional wellbeing, their spiritual growth, and the rearing of children.

#111   **What is a Priest?** *(Lost episode)*

#112   **The Woman Who Changed the World** *(Lost episode)*

#113   **What is the Mass?** *(Lost episode)*

1962

Fr. Keiser continued to write his commentary for the series, and presumably dramatic material as well, although no writing credits are recorded for the early seasons. Script consultants and story editors are sometimes credited. They include: Otis Carney, Hank Garson, E. Jack Neuman, Richard Breen, James Moser, and John Furia, Jr.

Joseph E. Connelly continued as Executive Producer for many of the early shows. The classic voice of Pat McGeehan provided narration for a number of years.

Many episodes in the early years of *Insight* are influenced by concern for the menace of totalitarian ideologies, i.e., the recent conflict with fascism and the growing threat of communist expansion. This is reflected in the words spoken over the show's opening credits at this time: "*Insight*: The religious principles underlying American democracy, the fundamental connection between faith and freedom."

#114 God & The Atheists

Producer: Donald Driscoll; Director: Jim Johnson

Cast: Eduardo Ciannelli

A critique is given of various forms of atheism: the "absolute" atheistic philosophies that brace up authoritarian movements; the "practical" atheism of those who ignore or are indifferent to God in favor of comfort or prestige; and the 'pseudo" atheism of those who reject religious hypocrisy but who may not in fact reject true notions of God.

#115 Beelzebub & The Bolsheviks

Producer: Don Driscoll; Director: Jim Johnson

Cast: Irene Dunn, Patrick McVey

Three people fight evil in their own ways: the Irish working man Matt Talbot fights his impulses toward alcohol through prayer; the German author Gertrude von Le Fort struggles with faith and conscience in the midst of Nazi oppression; and the American doctor Tom Dooley practices humanitarian work in Southeast Asia.

Irene Dunn in Beelzebub and the Bolsheviks

From Fr. Kieser's commentary in "Beelzebub and the Bolsheviks"

This country is only as strong as the individuals who compose it... We Americans must know what we believe and why we believe it. We must have a clearly articulated philosophy of freedom. If this battle [the Cold War] is to be won, we must be ready to sacrifice our comforts. We must be willing to suffer for our Christian, democratic ideals... There's much the individual can do. There's much you alone can do. I mean you can make your own private war on evil... You are to fight evil actions with good actions. Oppose hatred with love. Counter deceit with truth. And here you must begin with yourself... How long has it been since you've made an unsolicited donation to a worthy charity? When did you last volunteer to work on a community project? How do your business practices square with the justice and charity you owe your neighbor? Have you tolerated discrimination? Do you act as your brother's keeper? Do you go beyond that? I mean, are you your brother's brother?

#116 Vision of Freedom

Producer: Don Driscoll; Director: Jim Johnson

Cast: Patrick McVey

A mini documentary about the American Revolution. Thomas Jefferson envisions religious and political freedom for his new country, with an understanding that human rights and dignity are "unalienable."

#117 The Face of Tyranny

Producer: Don Driscoll; Director: Jim Johnson

Cast: Phil Carey, Audrey Dalton, Guy Prescott

The materialist and atheistic philosophies of Marx, Lenin, and Stalin are dramatized in stark contrast to the aspirations of the Hungarian freedom fighters who stood up to their Communist oppressors.

#118 Sinners, Inc

Producer: Don Driscoll; Director: Jim Johnson

Cast: Ann Blyth, Everett Sloane, Hans Conried, Clete Roberts

Lady Macbeth, Faustus, and a "Salesman" discuss their sins. The effects of their failures are seen to have both personal and social repercussions.

#119 Heart of Liberty

Producer: Don Driscoll; Director: Jim Johnson

Cast: Gene Raymond, Brian Keith, Lew Brown, Pat O'Malley

Colonists like William Brewster, William Penn, and Lord Baltimore offer their motives for coming to America. The role of churches and worship in American life is examined.

#120 Fabric of Freedom

Producer: Don Driscoll; Director: Jim Johnson

Cast: Dan O'Herlihy, Audrey Dalton, Guy Prescott, Wallace Rooney, John Ayres, Pat McGeehan, Jerry Hausner

The relationship of religion to moral and cultural health is discussed. An attempt is made to show what the average citizen can do to preserve America's strength.

#121 The Perennial Problem

Producer: Joseph Connelly; Director: Jim Johnson

Cast: Darryl Hickman, Christine White

Fr. Kieser gives his views on the spiritual basis of marriage and what makes for a successful marriage. Actors depict a young American couple moving through courtship and dealing with the issues of married life.

> From Fr. Kieser's commentary in "The Perennial Problem"
>
> Simone Weil, the great Jewish philosopher and thinker, puts it this way: "What makes physical desire so powerful in you is not a physical thing. It is powerful because you make it the vehicle of that which is most essential in you—the need for God." This is a very important point. Those who enter marriage thinking that human love in general and the marriage act in particular will solve all their problems and give them perfect fulfillment are going to be sadly disappointed. They make the mistake of Don Juan who looked for perfect happiness where it cannot be found. You have to be realistic here. You have been made for the face-to-face vision of God, and nothing short of that is going to fully content you. It's unwise to expect too much from a marriage. And yet you can work to spiritualize things. You can learn to look for the face of God in the soul of this person whom you love. And you can serve God by serving him or her.

#122 Christ, Caesar, Conscience

Producer: Don Driscoll; Director: Jim Johnson

Cast: MacDonald Carey, Pat McGeehan, Keith Vincent, John Ayres

James Madison writes the Constitution of the United States, forbidding an established religion and recognizing the sacredness of conscience in matters of religion.

#123 IOU My Brother

Producer: Don Driscoll; Director: Mike Cozzi

Cast: Victor Jory, Keith Vincent, Paul Picerni, Jerry Hausner, William Schallert

Social inequities spawned by the industrial revolution are examined. A case is made for the responsibility of labor, management, and government to work for just and humane conditions for workers and the poor.

#124 Cross in the Crisis

Producer: Don Driscoll; Director: Mike Cozzi

Cast: Jane Wyman, Raymond Massey, Marvin Miller, Ed Fleming

Three people come to grips with their belief in God's love for his creatures and the presence of evil in the world: Dr. Tanaka, a Japanese surgeon who survived the atomic bombing of Hiroshima; Edith Stein in the Auschwitz concentration camp; and Bishop Frank Ford in a Chinese communist prison.

> **Fr. Kieser's prologue to "Cross in the Crisis"**
>
> The problem faced by the inhabitants of Hiroshima is as old as human nature itself. For thousands upon thousands of years men have been asking: Why does God allow evil in the world he created? You and I would like to be able to ignore this problem, but we cannot. In different ways, under different guises, we must face it every day of our lives. Maybe a headache, the death of someone we love, or the selfishness of a friend that causes us to ask: Why did God create this kind of world? ... Why does God allow us to suffer? This is a problem, but it is more than a problem, it's a mystery. God understands it, but we do not. But still, we must deal with suffering.

> We must learn to face it with confidence and endure it with dignity. This is no easy job, but it can be accomplished. It will be accomplished if you learn from the experience of others...

#125 A Reason to live, A Reason to Die

Producer: Don Driscoll; Director: Dan Gingold; Writer: Ellwood Kieser.

Cast: Regis Toomey, Paul Picerni, Pat O'Malley

A man has an inner dialogue with himself and others about where to find purpose in life. Some propose pleasure and self-seeking as the answer. After finding those arguments wanting, he wonders if human life itself is futile. Then, in a dialogue with Fr. Kieser, he considers the Christian answer in the love of God and others.

#126 Ecce Homo

Producer: Joseph Connelly; Director: Phil Thorton

Narrator: Pat McGeehan

A mini documentary on the life of Christ, narrated over artworks. The episode features Fr. Keiser's personal invitation to faith.

1963

Shows continued to tackle issues and challenges brought on by modern life, like secularism, the Cold War, and divorce. This willingness to bring faith into dialogue with contemporary questions and anxieties became a hallmark of the series.

Starting this year, dramatic material took on more prominence as Fr. Kieser's commentary became more ancillary. Episodes now began with this introduction: "*Insight*: An exploration in depth of the spiritual conflicts of the twentieth century."

#127 The Sophomore

Producer: John Furia, Jr.; Director: Jim Johnson (?)

Cast: James MacArthur, Marlo Thomas, James Westerfield, Doreen Lang, William Schallert, Jim Stacy

A college sophomore contemplates his growing agnosticism and rejection of his parents' values. As he enters adulthood, his marriage and the birth of his child result in his reexamination of faith.

#128 The Edith Stein Story *(Lost episode)*

#129 The Phony

Producer: John Furia, Jr.; Director: Jim Johnson

Cast: Efrem Zimbalist Jr., Joan Leslie, Anne Helm

A salesman is good at his job and at keeping up with his social obligations. But he doesn't know who he is. He gets a wakeup call when his daughter exhibits his own conformism and lack of self-respect.

#130 Ragpicker

Producer: John Furia, Jr.; Director: Jim Johnson

Cast: Ricardo Montalbon, Herschel Bernardi, Eduard Franz, Christine White

Stories from suffering people during the post-World War II period in France are told. A priest struggles to make life better by giving people meaningful work to do.

#131 Operation Dignity

Producer: John Furia, Jr.; Director: Jim Johnson

Cast: Raymond Massey, Leo G. Carroll, William Lundigan, Gene Raymond

The story of three great popes of the twentieth century: Pope Leo XIII, Pope Pius X, and Pope Pius XII, whose great concern was the dignity of the human person.

#132 The Killer

Producer: John Furia, Jr.; Director: Jim Johnson

Cast: Frank Gorshim, Marvin Miller, Eduardo Ciannelli, Celia Lovsky, Jay Novello, Ann Jillian, Guy Prescott

The tragic yet hopeful story is told of St. Maria Goretti, one of the youngest saints ever to be canonized, and the man who killed her.

#133 Breakthrough

Producer: John Furia, Jr.; Director: Jim Johnson

Cast: Edmond O'Brien, Dick York, Bettye Ackerman, Charlene Salerno

A scientist invents a new and powerful laser but wishes to avoid the question of how his research will be used. His wife and his lab assistant cause him to examine his responsibility and the need for humility in the face of such power.

#134 The Conspirator

Producer: John Furia, Jr.; Director: Jack Shea

Cast: Dan O'Herlihy, Vera Miles, John Hoyt, George Macready, William Schallert

The true story of Claus von Stauffenberg: a drama of human conscience played out among rebel Nazi soldiers plotting to end the evil of the Third Reich.

> Fr. Kieser's prologue to "The Conspirator"
>
> Why is your conscience so important? Because it is the citadel of your freedom. Because it alone can direct the course of your life, determine your destiny, and bring you into close contact with God. Conscience is not feeling, or emotion, or sentiment. Conscience is the voice of reason telling you what is right and wrong. If your conscience is to function properly, it requires a knowledge of the objective moral principles revealed by God for the government of your life, a knowledge of the laws etched into your nature by God himself, a knowledge of your destiny and what it takes to fulfill it. The function of your conscience is to carry these principles into your everyday life, and to govern all your actions in accordance with them. It's not always easy to obey your conscience. Suffering and sacrifice may be the inevitable result. But you have no choice. The cost of disobedience is even greater. To ignore one's conscience is to abdicate one's dignity. To violate one's conscience dilutes one's freedom. To disobey one's conscience is to alienate oneself from God.

#135 The Tyrants

Producer: John Furia, Jr.; Director: Jim Johnson

Cast: Steve McNally, Werner Klemperer, Everett Sloane, John Marley

Imagined "interviews" are given by Stalin, Lenin, and Marx. Their economic theories are examined as well as the consequences of those theories for society and human rights.

#136 For Better or for Worse

Producer: John Furia, Jr.; Director: Jim Johnson

Cast: Robert Culp, Dolores Hart, Jorja Curtwright

A couple begins their engagement with superficial and selfish motives. After the are married, problems lead them to consider divorce, until they consider the deeper meaning of love and sacrifice.

#137 The Boy and the Bomb

Producer: John Furia, Jr.; Director: Jim Johnson

Cast: John Forsythe, Jeanne Crain, Jerry Mathers

In the face of the threat of nuclear war, a family discusses the bomb shelter they've built. The discussion turns to questions of religion and spirituality.

> **Fr. Kieser's prologue to "The Boy and the Bomb"**
>
> The threat of nuclear warfare has cast its long and sinister shadow into every corner of human life. At any moment, with the press of a button, or the snap of a finger, we could lose our friends, our possessions, even life itself. Death is never more than thirty seconds away. This isn't a pleasant realization. I don't think any of us enjoy thinking about it. But it is a fact. Sooner or later all of us must face the stark reality of death. If not from the bomb, then from disease, accident, or old age. The coming of death is certain; only the time is uncertain. Nuclear warheads and Intercontinental Ballistic Missiles merely make the problem more immediate.

> In the twentieth century, you need not be an engineer, a physicist, or a sociologist—but you must be a theologian. Our situation forces us to speculate about the meaning and purpose of human life, to seek some ultimate goal to aim at, beyond completing one day and looking forward to the dawn of the next. Quite spontaneously we ask: Where have I come from? Where am I going? Is death the end for me, or just the beginning? Must death be shunned, or can it be welcomed? What should I live for? What's the purpose of my life? These questions are central to every human life. But they are especially pressing for those of us who live in the shadow of the mushroom cloud.

#138 The Agitator

Producer: John Furia, Jr.; Director: Jack Shea

Cast: Ed Begley, Brian Keith, Ruth Hussey, Richard Kennedy, James Westerfield

Two hard-working newspaper men remember their quest to promote justice and humanism—but for very different reasons. One is motivated by his Catholic faith, the other by a secular ideology that becomes totalitarian.

> **Fr. Kieser's prologue to "The Agitator"**
>
> I call a man a humanist when he believes in the uniqueness of the human person, and the power of human reason, and the dignity of each member of the human race. I call a man a humanist when his thoughts and actions are motivated by a deep feeling for the corporate solidarity of the human family. Historically, humanism is the product of the Judeo-Christian tradition. It was developed by men like Aquinas, Erasmus, More, Bellarmine, Locke, Jefferson... For them, rights were inalienable because they were endowed by the creator, the mind accurate because it was reflective

> of the divine mind, freedom inviolable because man needs it to fulfill his destiny, which is to choose God... Their humanism was deeply rooted in their religious faith. During the last two hundred years, however, some of the western world's most respected minds rebelled against this tradition, and on the pretext of exalting reason, tried to tear humanism from its theological context and divorce it from all reference to God. For these men, religion is superstition; it alienates man from himself. Morality is oppressive, faith irrational, God the enemy of man. For them, man becomes his own ultimate end. The conflict between these two types of humanism has created the great crisis of the twentieth century...

#139 **The Martyr** *(Lost episode)*

1964

This year, the addition of more set and technical crew began to elevate the show's production values. Writing changes were also made. Previously, script consultants assisted Fr. Kieser in writing the stories and his teaching segments. Now, individual writers were given script credits, and the dramas themselves took center stage. Fr. Kieser's commentary continued in brief introductions, intervals, conclusions, or was simply omitted.

The accomplished television writer, director, and producer John Meredyth Lucas began a long association with the show with his script about a marriage in crisis: "Prometheus Bound."

#140 **The Prisoner**

Producer: Jack Shea; Director: David O. McDearmon; Writer: E. Sarsfield Waters

Cast: Jack Klugman, Werner Klemperer, Robert H. Harris, Dehl Berti, Dan Tobin, Frank Maxwell, Martin Brandt, Penny O'Donnell

In retaliation for a prisoner's escape, a commandant at Auschwitz selects one of the remaining inmates to be starved to death. Another prisoner, Fr. Maximillian Kolbe, offers to take the condemned man's place, which has a profound effect on the saved man.

Jack Klugman in The Prisoner

#141 The Capitalist

Producer: Jack Shea; Director: Sutton Roley; Writer: William Donnelly

Cast: Henry Silva, Thomas Gomez, Paul Picerni, Patricia Breslin, Carlos Rivas, Carmelita Acosta

A Latin American union leader gets caught up between two extremes: communists who enforce atheism and authoritarianism, and capitalists who ignore people's rights in order to benefit themselves.

Paul Picerni in The Capitalist

Fr. Kieser's prologue to "The Capitalist"

The communist attack upon personal freedom and the democratic process is particularly bitter in Latin America. In many parts of the southern hemisphere, communist agitators seek to infiltrate the organs of society so as to preach their doctrine of atheistic world revolution. The communists consider class conflict inevitable. As long as men are free to own property, they say, those who do will exploit those who don't. But when the misery and degradation of the proletariat becomes bad enough, they will revolt, seize the means of production, and the result will be communism. It alone, they say, can solve the problems of society. The communists consider this a predetermined historical sequence; but they seek to hasten it. When class conflict exists, they seek to abet it; when it does not, they seek to create it. In promoting their cause, the communists have many allies, but none more powerful than the irresponsible capitalist, who is so jealous of his own rights that he forgets the rights of others. These men divorce individual freedom from public service. They see the value of private property for themselves, but they feel no obligation to help other people to enjoy its benefits. Without knowing it, they are the best friends the communists have.

#142 The Urchin

Producer: Jack Shea; Director: Michael J. Kane; Writer: John Fante

Cast: Don Gordon, Jamie Farr, Joe de Santis, Jay Novello, Manuel Padilla, Jr., Larry Domasin, Rafael Lopez, Roger Mobley

A priest in post-war Naples reaches out to the abandoned street kids that fill the city. First, he must win their trust and then convince them that they have a future.

Don Gordon in The Urchin

"In one's career, you always have those dry moments. I hadn't worked for quite a while. I get this phone call... Fr. Ellwood Kieser does a show on Sunday called *Insight*. He would have famous people, writers, directors, actors, do the show. And he would pay minimum. He called and wanted me to play an Italian priest... They said, now Jamie, just be careful: The last day of shooting, Fr. Kieser will come down in front of everybody and he'll hand you the check. And he expects a lot of people to say, 'No, that's all right, Father, you keep it.' So, here's what you've got to do: When he hands you the check... you say, 'No, that's all right, you keep it.' Then he'll say, 'No, no, Jamie, I want you to have it.' And you'll say, 'No, no, that's all right,' and he'll say, 'No, I want you to have it,' and on the third one, take the check! ... So, it's the final day of shooting... Fr. Kieser comes out and says, 'Jamie, here's your check.' I say, 'No, no. Father, that's all right, you keep it.' He says, 'All Right.' ... He didn't go to the third one!"[5]

Jamie Farr

#143 Diary of a Beatnik

Producer: Jack Shea; Director: Jack Shea; Writer: John T. Dugan

Cast: Don Gordon, Carolyn Kearney, Skip Homeier, Coleen Gray

A writer in Greenwich Village wrestles with belief in God. His girlfriend gives him an ultimatum: God or her. He searches for the answer that will make him whole.

#144 The Hermit

Producer: Jack Shea; Director: Richard Bennett; Writer: Richard Breen

Cast: Efrem Zimbalist, Jr., Jane Wyman, Maurice Marsac, Peter Leeds, Henry Corden, Henry Beckman

The story is told of Charles de Foucauld, a French aristocrat who became a humble monk and chose to live among the poor in the Moroccan desert. During World War I, a local chieftain orders him to leave or be killed.

Jane Wyman in The Hermit

#145 The Porous Curtain

Producer: Jack Shea; Director: Gene Law; Writer: David Moessinger

Cast: Richard Egan, Pat Crowley, Lawrence Dobkin, Dehl Berti, Ivy Bethune, Theodore Marcuse

An American photographer touring the Soviet Union must cope with his faith in a society attempting to obliterate religion. He encounters people looking for something beyond this world to enrich their lives.

Richard Egan in The Porous Curtain

#146 Prometheus Bound

Producer: Jack Shea; Director: Hal Cooper; Writer: John Meredyth Lucas

Cast: Mark Richman, Vera Miles, David White, Bek Nelson

An alcoholic man having an affair and his pregnant wife must deal with their unhappy marriage and the birth of their mentally disabled child.

Vera Miles, Mark Richman, and crew on the set of Prometheus Bound

> **Fr. Kieser's prologue to "Prometheus Bound"**
>
> Freedom is at once the most wonderous and terrifying of human powers. It is wonderous because it is the power to love, to surrender oneself to God as he lives in other people, to make one's life a service of them. Freedom is terrifying because it is the power to say no to love, to make egotistical gratification the sum total of one's existence, to close in on oneself in an ecstasy of self-adoration. This is the basic choice that faces every human being: to love, or not to love; to live for God or to live for oneself; to open out in the service of others, or to close in behind the four walls of one's own ego...

#147 The Lovers

Producer: Jack Shea; Director: Paul Stanley; Writer: John T. Kelley

Cast: Nina Shipman, Pat Harrington, Abigail Shelton

A secretary in love is forced to choose between her conscience and the demands of her boyfriend. She comes to regret choices made out of fear of losing his love.

#148 Boss Toad

Producer: Jack Shea; Director: Gordon Wiles; Writer: Dehl Franke

Cast: Ann Sothern, Brian Keith, Richard Eyer, Cheryl Holdridge

A teenage boy is caught between the disciplinary restrictions imposed by his well-meaning parents and the selfish whims of his girlfriend, whose parents don't believe in discipline. He comes to accept the limitations imposed on him and asks her to do the same.

#149 The Invincible Weapon

Producer: Jack Shea; Director: Arthur Hiller; Writer: Louis Robinson

Cast: Ivan Dixon, William Marshall, Gloria Calomee, Robert DeCoy, Davis Roberts, Sandy Lewis, Keg Johnson, Robert Fortier

A high school football coach believes only violent measures will get results, both in civil rights demonstrations and in his games. When the resentment and vengeance he preaches to his team results in the serious injury of a player, he changes his mind about how to fight for racial justice.

> Fr. Kieser's prologue to "The Invincible Weapon"
>
> Our free way of life is built upon the proposition that each and every member of the human race Is possessed of infinite dignity. All men are created equal, Jefferson wrote. They are endowed by their creator with certain inalienable rights, among which are life, liberty, and the pursuit of happiness. All possess these rights. They enjoy this equality simply and solely because they are human beings, made in the image and likeness of God. Their race and color have nothing to do with it. Man's rights and dignity are inalienable precisely because they've been endowed by their creator. No individual or group has a right to deny these rights or compromise this dignity. To do so, is to violate an order established by God himself. Here in America, these principles have been universally acknowledged. But they have not been universally applied. A portion of our population has too frequently been asked to accept a position of second-class citizenship. Because of their color, they have too often been denied the jobs, the schools, and housing necessary for the maintenance of human dignity. They've been asked to wait until some future time for the enjoyment of their God-given rights. Quite rightly, they have gotten tired of waiting. And so, they have begun to act. But how? What means do they use to secure their God-given rights?

#150 The Kid Show

Producer: Jack Shea; Director: Paul Stanley; Writer: Carole O'Brien

Cast: Jack Klugman, Brian Keith, Pat Cardi

A young boy who witnesses an attempted suicide enters a carnival fantasy that exposes him to different characters and approaches to life. They seem to battle for his soul.

Pat Cardi, Jack Klugman, and Brian Keith in The Kid Show

#151 Cross of Russia

Producer: Jack Shea; Director: Ted Post; Writer: John T. Dugan

Cast: Steve Forrest, Guy Stockwell, Brian Keith, Joe de Santis, Joe Higgins, Jimmy Hayes, Reed Sherman

Inspired by true events during the Bolshevik persecution of religious groups in the 1920's, the Metropolitan of the Russian Orthodox Church and an archpriest of the Catholic Church in Russia stand accused of capital crimes for practicing their religion.

Steve Forrest in Cross of Russia

#152 Brothers in the Dark

Producer: Jack Shea; Director: Ted Post; Writer: E. Sarsfield Waters

Cast: Marion Ross, Paul Richards, Skip Homeier, Jacques Aubuchon

In 1938, a New York City man struggles to keep up with the communist party's demands on him as a party member. He can no longer reconcile those demands with the ideals of peace and justice he so deeply believes in.

"Myself and another writer, John Furia, were both found by Bud Kieser. He brought us in to see if we could help him do some television shows. We were interested in doing that for a good purpose, because we thought that a lot of the so-called religious television was just terrible. So, we decided we would try to help him make some good shows. Of course, there was no money involved, so John organized writers and I organized directors and we talked these people into working for free, for a show, for the good of the world. And a lot of people responded... It really brought a lot of people together...

"I was trying to do a series at one point for the University of Judaism. I was producing, and I complained to them that I wasn't able to find a Jewish writer or director to work on it. And they said, 'Of course not, you've got them all over there on the Catholic show!' So, then I realized we had made a major impact..."[6]

Jack Shea, Producer/Director

#153 Fisher of Men

(Not technically part of the *Insight* series, this show was a vocational recruitment film on behalf of the Paulist Fathers, which may have been broadcast in some places.)

Producer: Ellwood Kieser; Director: Jack Shea; Writer: Ellwood Kieser

Cast: Brian Kelly, Brian Keith, Laura Devon, Jim Westerfield, Audrey Dalton, Richard Eyer, Lawrence Dobkin, Greg Morris, Jim Callahan, Joe Higgins, Henry Beckman, Edward Faulkner

A day in the life of a busy parish priest is presented. A man with doubts, needs, joys, and sorrows seeks to serve God by serving people.

1965

The show seemed to break new ground in 1965 in its willingness to wrestle with the moral implications of contemporary social problems. Gilbert Ralston's "Locusts Have No King," a dramatic look at one man's fight against local civic corruption, and John D. F. Black's "The Woodpile," a treatment of racism in the workplace, are examples.

Performances of note include: Vera Miles in John Meredyth Lucas' "The World, the Campus, and Sr. Lucy Ann;" Albert Salmi in John D.F. Black's and Gerry Day's "With a Long Gray Beard;" Robert Lansing in Richard Breen's "Thunder in Munich;" and Beverly Garland and John Dehner in James Moser's "A Thief Named Dismas."

The narration over the opening credits of the series changed this year to: "*Insight*: Stories of spiritual conflict in the twentieth century."

#154 The Thousand Mile Journey *(Lost episode)*

Producer: Uncertain; Director: Uncertain; Writer: John Meredyth Lucas

Cast: Sally Kellerman, others unknown

To her mother's disbelief, a young socialite who wants to change the world decides to help the destitute by living in the slums.

Sally Kellerman in The Thousand Mile Journey

#155 The Dog That Bit You

Producer: Jack Shea; Director: Lamar Caselli; Writer: John T. Kelly

Cast: Brian Keith, Beverly Garland, Edward Binns, Sara Seegar

A newspaper man who lacks confidence in his writing ability attempts to find courage and inspiration in drinking. After getting fired for missing an important deadline, he turns to AA for help.

Brian Keith in The Dog That Bit You

Fr. Kieser's prologue to "The Dog That Bit You"

We are rational animals; yet we often act irrationally. We are free; yet we suffer from various compulsions. We are spiritual beings; yet on occasion we find ourselves enslaved by physical desire. All of us struggle with this interior contradiction. The alcoholic must struggle with it in a very special way, for he has contracted a disease which seriously compromises his dignity. He experiences a physical need for alcohol. He also experiences a mental compulsion to satisfy that need regardless of the consequences. Sometimes the consequences are dire indeed. Not infrequently, the alcoholic disrupts his family, jeopardizes his job, and destroys his health. He knows these things are the result of his drinking. He regrets them, he feels great remorse, yet he seems unable to stop. This is an important point: most alcoholics are incapable of helping themselves. Sheer will power is not enough to solve their problem. Does this mean their case is hopeless? Are they condemned to self-destruction? It doesn't mean that. It does mean the alcoholic must look beyond himself for the solution of his problem.

#156 Stranger in My Shoes

Producer: James Loren; Director: Hal Cooper; Writers: Gerry Day, B.W. Sandefur

Cast: Efrem Zimbalist, Jr., Julie Adams, Joe Flynn, Cliff Norton, William Bakewell, Andrew Prine, June Dayton, Regina Gleason

A former English professor who left his teaching job for a large salary as a leading advertising executive, struggles to live with a superficial set of values. He realizes that material success has not brought him self-fulfillment.

Efrem Zimbalist, Jr. in Stranger in My Shoes

#157 Locusts Have No King

Producer: James Loren; Director: Ted Post; Writer: Gilbert Ralston

Cast: William Shatner, Geraldine Brooks, Kent Smith, Henry Beckman, Walter Brooke, Don Ross, Hoyt Wertz, Charles Dugdale

A man's moral compass requires him to defy the powerful and corrupt interests in his town. When they threaten his family, he must make a wrenching decision.

Geraldine Brooks and William Shatner in Locusts Have No King

Fr. Kieser's prologue to "Locusts Have No King"

The fact that you have an eternal and spiritual destiny does not mean that the affairs of time and the concerns of earth are not important. Nothing could be further from the truth. What you do in time determines how you spend eternity. You achieve your destiny in the next world only by doing the will of God in this one. What does this mean? Fidelity to principle, obedience to the law of love, unselfish involvement in the service of others. I'm my brother's keeper. Doesn't this also make me society's keeper? I am responsible for its welfare. I am duty-bound to seek its health. God expects me to do all I can to construct a society conducive to the realization of man's spiritual and eternal destiny. This is no easy job. Modern social life is very complex. It's so easy to say: I'll take care of myself; let somebody else worry about the common good. This is a temptation. It must be resisted. The common good is of common concern. All are bound to seek it. But how, and at what price?

#158 Murder in the Family

Producer: John Furia, Jr.; Director: Richard Bennett; Writer: Harry Julian Fink

Cast: Guy Stockwell, Phyllis Love, Stephen Coit, Frederic Downs, Robert Duggan, Tim Graham, Jacques Denbeaux

An immigrant's son wants to provide his wife and future family with all the things he never had. When his wife gets pregnant, and he feels unable to adequately support a child, he chooses a path that gnaws at the fabric of their marriage.

Guy Stockwell in Murder in the Family

#159 Thunder in Munich

Producer: James Loren; Director: Marc Daniels; Writer: Richard Breen

Cast: Robert Lansing, Berkeley Harris, Chet Stratton, Ford Rainey, Joan Swift, Russell Collins, Kent Smith, Jacques Denbeaux

The true story of Rupert Meier, a German Jesuit who fought the Nazi ideology from the pulpit. When he openly denounces the regime, he is arrested and sent to a concentration camp where he dies.

#160 The World, the Campus, and Sr. Lucy Ann

Producer: Jack Shea; Director: Richard Bennett; Writer: John Meredyth Lucas

Cast: Vera Miles, Andrew Prine, Eduard Franz, Nina Shipman, Herbert Anderson

A nun studying in a secular university takes a drama class and clashes with two of her fellow students over the meaning of love and the value of her own vocation.

Vera Miles in The World, the Campus, and Sr. Lucy Ann

#161 The Fire Within

Producer: James Loren; Director: John Peyser; Writer: E. Sarsfield Waters

Cast: Brian Keith, Leslie Parrish, Carroll O'Conner, Linda Leighton

A man, upset with his life, plans to leave his wife for a different woman. He collapses and has a vision of being "stuck" with his lover in a luxurious hotel room.

#162 **The Woodpile**

Producer: John Furia, Jr.; Director: John Rich; Writer: John D. F. Black

Cast: Charles Aidman, Gerald Mohr, Vaughn Taylor, Ben Wright, Greg Morris, Robert Brubaker, Jan Burrell

A well-qualified black man's application for a top executive position at a large electronics firm is denied due to the racial prejudice of the firm's board of directors.

Gerald Mohr in The Woodpile

#163 **With a Long Gray Beard**

Producer: Uncertain; Director: Uncertain; Writers: John D.F. Black, Gerry Day

Cast: Albert Salmi, Patricia Barry, Don Gordon

A high-strung super salesman works too hard, drinks too much, and his wife is leaving him. Consistently unheeding other people's concern for him, he ends up in a hospital room fighting for redemption.

#164 The Right-Handed World

Producer: John Furia, Jr.; Director: Lamar Caselli; Writer: Michael Gleason

Cast: James Farentino, Barbara Baldavin, Bert Freed, Richard Bull, Sanford Lewis, Kim Hamilton

A college student plunges into social work despite his family's objections. When he becomes discouraged, a professor reminds him that by serving others, he is serving God.

#165 *(Lost episode)*

#166 A Thief Named Dismas

Producer: John Furia, Jr.; Director: Richard Bennett; Writer: James Moser

Cast: Beverly Garland, John Dehner, Marge Redmond, Jennifer Crier

A wealthy woman who has lived by seeking only material and sensual gratification, plans an escape with a married man. In desperation, she comes to realize her need to take responsibility for her life.

#167 A Thief Named Dismas, Part II *(Lost episode)*

Beverly Garland in A Thief Named Dismas, Part II

1966

This year, *Insight* began broadcasting in color.

The series' unflinching look at the spiritual dimension of hot button social issues continued in classic episodes like Rod Serling's "The Hate Syndrome," a disconcerting treatment of anti-Semitism; and Richard Breen's "Don't Let Me Catch You Praying," a searing indictment of suburban racism.

John T. Duggan's "Trial by Fire," set in a mythic time and place, nonetheless was evocative for a country fighting a troubling war in Vietnam.

#168 Don't Elbow Me Off the Earth

Producer: James Loren; Director: Hal Cooper; Writer: Theodore Apstein

Cast: Brian Keith, Beverly Garland, James Gregory, Rick Kelman, Philip Abbott, Stella Garcia

A father judges his neighbor for accepting unemployment checks instead of taking the first job that is offered to him. When he himself loses his job, he questions where his true value is found.

#169 The Least of My Brothers

Producer: James Loren; Director: Richard Bennett; Writer: John Meredyth Lucas

Cast: Beau Bridges, Don Penny, Brooke Bundy, Kerwin Matthews, Rafael Campos, Carlos Rivas, Augustina Brunetti

A college student who feels his life is devoid of meaning rejects his religion and campus life to join the Peace Corps. Although committed to serving the destitute in Latin America, he becomes discouraged by the lack of concrete results.

> Fr. Kieser's commentary on "The Least of My Brothers"
>
> We have been called an anxious people. I don't think we have any monopoly on anxiety, but we are anxious, there's no doubt about that. Paul Tillich, the great Protestant theologian, says that most of our anxiety is caused by a feeling of futility. Sometimes our lives seem to make no sense, and so we look for some goal, some purpose to give meaning to all else. Until we find it, we should be anxious... Simone Weil, the very perceptive Jewish thinker, says that the need for meaning is the deepest desire of the human heart. I have felt this need, so have you. We have felt it every day of our lives. I wish I could tell you that there was some simple, easy way to satisfy this need once and for all, but I can't. Giving your life meaning and purpose is a daily challenge, and it's never easy. But I can tell you that it's bound up with contacting God. 'Thou hast made us for thyself, O Lord,' St. Augustine prays, 'And our

hearts are restless until they rest in Thee.' But how is God to be contacted? Sometimes he seems so very far away. He may seem far away, but he's not. He's as close as the closest human being. I believe that God can be found in the pain and need of our fellow human creatures. In loving them, we're loving God. In serving them, we're serving him. In reaching out to help them, we contact God. And to contact God is to discover the real meaning, the true purpose of our lives.

#170 Why Sparrows Fall

Producer: James Loren; Director: Paul Nickell; Writer: Adele Strassfield

Cast: Vera Miles, Lloyd Bochner, Walter Brooke, Jaques Aubuchon, Frank Maxwell

A famous stage actress, facing a terminal illness, tries to lose herself in work. She must finally come to terms with her incompleteness and guilt.

Lloyd Bochner and Vera Miles in Why Sparrows Fall

#171 The Oleander Years

Producer: James Loren; Director: Robert Butler; Writer: Leon Tokatyan

Cast: Robert Lansing, Geraldine Brooks

An apparently happy couple on vacation find their marriage has become an empty shell; yet the possibility of intimacy still presents itself.

Robert Lansing and Geraldine Brooks in The Oleander Years

#172 The Hate Syndrome

Producer: James Loren; Director: Marc Daniels; Writer: Rod Serling

Cast: Eduard Franz, James Beggs, Harold Stone, Davis Roberts, Lincoln Demyan

A young American Nazi, ironically a fallen-away Jew, collides verbally and physically with his former Hebrew teacher.

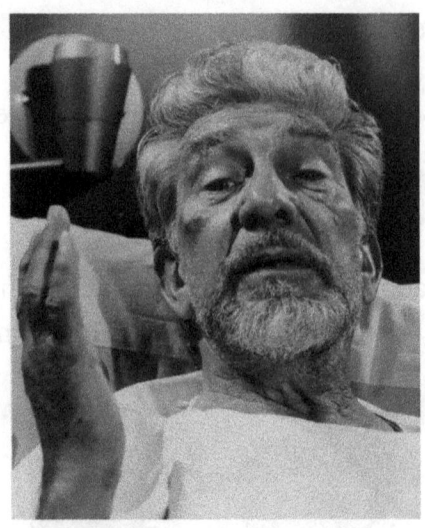

Eduard Franz in The Hate Syndrome

Fr. Kieser's commentary on "The Hate Syndrome"

Our century has witnessed great triumphs of the human spirit. But it has also witnessed human degradation of incredible magnitude. Dachau, Lidice, Warsaw, Budapest, Dallas, Selma. The list is long enough to make most of us sick. In exasperation we ask: Why do men hate? Why do some men need someone to hate? These are good questions. We should ask them. But we shouldn't be self-righteous. For the ones who did these things are not unlike ourselves. The seeds of hatred reside in every human heart. I could be a hater. So could you. This is not a pleasant thought. But it is a true one... I'm not going to tell you that loving is easy. It's not. But I can tell you that loving will enable you to tap a new kind of power. Love those who hate you. Smile at those who scorn you. Do good to those who abuse you. And notice what happens. Your enemy's hatred is disarmed, and ultimately it will be destroyed. You think I'm talking idealistically? I dare you to try it. You'll see. Love is the most powerful force in the world.

#173 The Governor's Mansion

Producer: James Loren; Director: Ted Post; Writer: Harry Julian Fink

Cast: Leif Erickson, Henry Beckman, Richard Erdman, Barry Atwater, Carolyn Conwell

A corrupt governor pressures an elected judge to facilitate a divorce he doesn't want the media to know about. Others are left to struggle with the implications.

#174 The Coffee House

Producer: James Loren; Director: Lamar Caselli; Writers: Walter Bodlander, Barry Oringer

Cast: Efrem Zimbalist, Jr., Dennis Safren, Dort Clark, Joe Higgins, Bibi Boles, Peter Dunhill, Steve Nesbit, Brian Dunne

An ex-cop opens a coffee shop where a local gang usually hangs out. He tries to recruit the gang leader to help run the business and not control the neighborhood through fear.

#175 The Truth about Time

Producer: James Loren; Director: Bill Hobin; Writer: Dave Moessenger, E. Sarsfield Waters

Cast: John Forsythe, John Gentri, John Doucette, Robert Brubaker, Bob Duggan

A hard-bitten war correspondent attempts to communicate with his sister's convicted killer. Through several prison visits, he comes to realize how empty and unhappy the other man's life is.

#176 Don't Let Me Catch You Praying

Producer: James Loren; Director: Richard Bennett; Writer: Richard Breen

Cast: Edward Andrews, Ruth Warrick, Philip Abbott, Robert des Londe, Henry Corden, Mimi Dillard, Sean McClory, Chet Stratton, Dick Wilson, Bob Duggan

A man who considers himself a pillar of the Church and a champion of civil rights is deeply shaken when he learns a black family plans to move into his neighborhood.

> From Fr. Kieser's prologue to "Don't Let Me Catch You Praying"
>
> Like every other good thing, religion can be misused. It can be perverted. And when it is, the results are monstrous... Authentic religious practice will be marked by humility and compassion. Any religious practice that does not express its love for God in the unselfish service of others is false. It is repugnant to God.

#177 Trial by Fire

Associate Producer: Neil T. Maffeo; Director: Buzz Kulik; Writer: John T. Duggan

Cast: Bradford Dillman, Ricardo Montalban, Jeff Corey, John van Dreelen, Pippa Scott

The conscience of an American combat pilot will not allow him to obey his superiors. Military and family members do all they can to change his mind.

#178 Snow in Summer

Associate Producer: Neil T. Maffeo; Director: Hal Cooper; Writer: Dehl Franke

Cast: Joan Freeman, Norman Fell, Richard Evans, D'urville Martin, Shannon Farnon, Ron Trujillo

A salesgirl confronts her own loneliness after becoming addicted to drugs and losing her job and self-respect.

#179 Politics Can Become a Habit

Associate Producer: Neil T. Maffeo; Director: Mel Ferber; Writer: Bernard Abbene

Cast: Peter Fonda, Diane Baker, Anne Seymore, Joyce Van Patten, Alan Hewitt, Paulene Myers, Katie Sweet

A nun who teaches sociology begins to question the value of her life and work when a young agitator confronts her about her lack of practical knowledge about the problems of the poor.

#180 Who Has Ever Seen Xanadu

Associate Producer: Neil T. Maffeo; Director: Richard Bennett; Writer: James Moser

Cast: Arthur O'Connell, John Hoyt, Ann Elder, Pat Cardi, Martin Brooks, Bunny Henning, Terri Garr, Arthur Batanides, Robert Moser

A wealthy man isolates himself and his children in a remote mansion. After his daughter runs away, he seeks the help of his carefree brother. The family learns a harsh lesson about the futility of trying to run from the world.

Arthur O'Connell in Who Has Ever Seen Xanadu

1967

The show began to experiment with on-location shooting for brief segments.

Additionally, the serious streak of the show was broken by Carol Sobieski's "A Funny Thing Happened" – a humorous treatment of its psychological and existential themes. John T. Duggan's post-apocalyptic allegory "The Nitty Gritty Once and Future Now" might be considered the series' first foray into science fiction.

#181 Some Talk About Pool Rooms and Gin Mills

Producer: John Furia, Jr.; Director: Hal Cooper; Writer: William McGivern

Cast: James MacArthur, Donald Mitchell, Kim Hamilton, Robert DeCoy, Barbara Baldavin, Joe Higgins

A white thug is forced to learn something about brotherhood when he has to live with an African American family while hiding out from the police.

#182 A Funny Thing Happened on the Way

Producer: John Furia, Jr.; Director: John Newland; Writer: Carol Sobieski

Cast: Norma Crane, Paul Carr, Norman Fell

A couple miss connections at an airport because she goes the wrong direction, and he goes in no direction. The complaint department tries to get them to help each other find a purpose for their lives.

Norman Fell and Norma Crane in A Funny Thing Happened on the Way

#183 Seed of Dissent

Producer: John Furia, Jr.; Director: Paul Stanley; Writer: John Meredyth Lucas

Cast: Robert Lansing, Marion Ross, Terry Burnham, Ed Asner, Henry Corden

A father is shattered when he finds out his daughter has been raped and is pregnant. He can't reconcile his anguish with his faith.

Robert Lansing and Terry Burnham in Seed of Dissent

#184 Madam

Producer: John Furia, Jr.; Director: Sherman Marks; Writer: Harry Julian Fink

Cast: Vera Miles, Jeff Hunter, Robert Cornthwaite, Debby Larsen

A woman who sells a pornographic magazine reveals her own hatred of sex, women, and herself when her handsome assistant falls in love and is sickened by what their work represents.

#185 Man in the Middle

Producer: John Furia, Jr.; Director: James Sheldon; Writer: John T. Kelley

Cast: Steve Forrest, Beverly Garland, Bernie Hamilton, Lyle Bettger, Mark Allen, Mae Clark, Bob Duggan

A small-town mayor tries to mediate between white bigots and a mob trying to overthrow the white power structure. As in previous episodes dealing with racism, Fr. Kieser's commentary strongly endorses the civil rights movement and affirms the choice for non-violence.

Steve Forrest and Beverly Garland in Man in the Middle

From Fr. Kieser's commentary for "Man in the Middle"

The world we live in is changing at break-neck speed. Social structures that we have taken for granted are being swept away and new ones are being erected in their place. This is sometimes disconcerting and on occasion painful. Change often is, even good change. In a democratic society, social progress is propelled by free discussion and the development of a consensus. On occasion, it is hurried forward by protest and peaceful demonstration. But what if the *status quo* refuses to change?... The great Pope John used to speak a great deal about the necessity of reading the 'signs of the times.' By that he meant that the will of God could be discerned in the needs and aspirations of our fellow human beings... God created the human race as one family. That's the way he wants it...

> Any cleavage in the human family based on race, any barrier created by prejudice, is contrary to God's plan. It's offensive to him. How can you call God your Father unless you are ready and anxious to accept all men as your brothers?

#186 Hang-Up

Producer: John Furia, Jr.; Director: Paul Stanley; Writer: E. Sarsfield Waters

Cast: Chris Robinson, Barbara Anderson

A young couple in love face a crisis of conscience when they feel like sleeping together but want to honor their relationship as it is. Communication and caring result in deeper understanding and a desire to move forward in love.

#187 A Small Statistic

Producer: John Furia, Jr.; Director: Robert Butler; Writer: Leon Tokatyan

Cast: James Stacy, Davey Davison, Katherine Bard, Ron Soble, Helen Kleeb, Anna Navarro, Susan Crane, Janee Michele, Ned Glass, Mike Pataki

The complacent happiness of a young couple is shattered when their first child dies at birth. A nun at the hospital tries to accompany them through their grief.

Davey Davison and James Stacy in A Small Statistic

Fr. Kieser's prologue to "A Small Statistic"

Human love is the most beautiful thing in all of creation. It can give you great joy and fulfillment. But is it ever quite enough? Can you completely satisfy each other's needs—all of them, I mean? Can you shield each other from pain and guilt? Can the two of you totally control your own lives? Or are you subject to some higher law? Must you reach through each other, yet beyond each other for the happiness and fulfillment you require?

#188 The Nitty Gritty Once and Future Now

Producer: John Furia, Jr.; Director: Richard Bennett; Writer: John T. Duggan

Cast: Patricia Harty, Richard Elkins, Lloyd Bochner, Joseph Campanella

Three survivors of the Third World War are astonished by the arrival of a mysterious stranger who offers them a way out of their trapped existence. They reject him, but then search for his path.

Lloyd Bochner, Patricia Harty, and Richard Elkins in
The Nitty Gritty Once and Future Now

#189 A Dry Commitment

Producer: John Furia, Jr.; Director: Alex March; Writer: Donald Munson

Cast: Joseph Campanella, William Marshall, Richard Angarola, Jannee Michele, Jason Wingreen, Noel Souza, Parki Singh, Maria Diaz, A.J. Singh

During a deadly famine in India, an American journalist learns that supplies are being kept from the masses by corrupt government officials. He must decide between his profession and involving himself in the plight of the people.

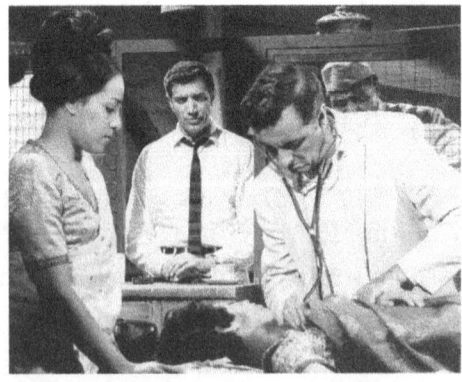

*Jannee Michele, Joseph Campanella,
and Jason Wingreen in* A Dry Commitment

#190 Where Were You During the Battle of the Bulge, Kid

Producer: John Furia, Jr.; Director: Seymour Robbie; Writer: William McGivern

Cast: Tim O'Connor, Robert Doyle, Michael Burns, Jacqueline Scott, Wesley Addy, Dan Barton

A father and son experience a generation gap in the way they approach school, work, and society. They have difficulty communicating until they find themselves facing identical problems.

Robert Doyle, Jacqueline Scott, and Michael Burns in Where Were You During the Battle of the Bulge, Kid

#191 The Whole Damn Human Race and One More

Producer: John Furia, Jr.; Director: Ralph Senensky; Writer: David Karp

Cast: Mark Richman, Jack Albertson, Barbara Hershey, June Dayton, Than Wyenn

A dedicated humanitarian loves the whole world but neglects his own daughter. His brother tries to teach him that love is most real when shared with the ones closest to us.

Barbara Hershey and Jack Albertson in
The Whole Damn Human Race and One More

#192 Fat Hands and a Diamond Ring

Producer: John Furia, Jr.; Director: Arthur Hiller; Writer: John D. F. Black

Cast: Barry Sullivan, Celeste Holm, Martin Milner, Howard Morris, Gigi Perreau, Mary Jackson, Oliver McGowan, Ned Glass, Ted Cassidy, Barry Cahill, Harold Gould

A self-seeking lawyer presides over a circus in his law office and the courtroom. He can ignore the demands of justice until his own home is shattered by his complacency and avoidance of reality.

Celeste Holme in Fat Hands and a Diamond Ring

#193 All the Little Plumes in Pain

Producer: John Furia, Jr.; Director: John Newland; Writer: Donald Munson

Cast: Guy Stockwell, Andrew Prine, Celia Kaye, Robert Crawford, Jr., Robert Doyle

Two worlds collide when a young lawyer enters a hippie shop in San Francisco in search of a client's runaway daughter. She has to decide how love will overcome fear.

1968

Insight continued to explore the personal, interpersonal, and social turmoil of the 1960s with episodes like John Bloch's "Three Cornered Flag," about the costs of the Vietnam war, and William Peter Blatty's "Watts Made Out of Thread," a theological comedy of redemption. The encounter group movement of the time is treated in James Moser's "The 34th Hour," and the impact of popular secularist ideologies is tackled in E. Sarsfield Waters' "The Late Great God."

#194 *(Lost episode)*

#195 He Lived with Us, He Ate with Us, What Else, Dear?

Producer: John Meredyth Lucas; Director: Seymour Robbie; Writer: William McGivern

Cast: Efrem Zimbalist, Jr., Guy Stockwell, Patricia Barry, Robert Random

An alienated father and son live in isolated worlds. When the son commits a crime, they find a way to bridge their differences and face a hard reality.

Efrem Zimbalist, Jr., Patricia Barry, and Robert Random in
He Lived with Us, He Ate with Us, What Else, Dear?

#196 Mummy

Producer: John Meredyth Lucas; Director: Lamont Johnson; Writer: Carol Sobieski

Cast: Arlene Golonka, Ike Williams

A young, harried mother hates the limitations imposed by her children. Feeling desperate and guilty, she fantasizes about escaping until she actually gets the chance to do so.

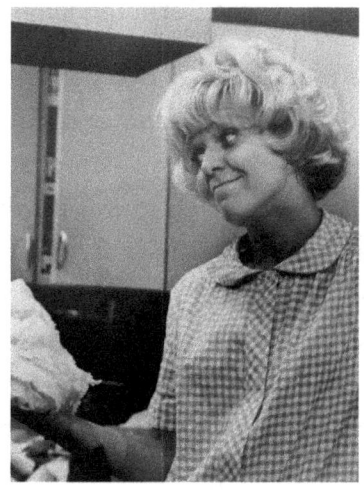

Arlene Golonka in Mummy

#197 Look Back to the Garden

Producer: John Meredyth Lucas; Director: John Meredyth Lucas; Writer: John Meredyth Lucas

Cast: Dwayne Hickman, Sharon Farrell, Donnelly Rhodes, D'urville Martin

A young couple having an affair are confronted with the effects of sexual license. Together they finally engage the possibility of intimacy and commitment.

#198 Three Cornered Flag

Producer: John Meredyth Lucas; Director: Paul Stanley; Writer: John Bloch

Cast: Ruth Warrick, Beau Bridges, Meredith MacRae, Ed Asner, Robert Karnes

The family of a soldier killed in Vietnam prepare to attend his funeral. They review their impact on the boy's decision to go to war.

> **Fr. Kieser's prologue to "Three Cornered Flag"**
>
> War may not be the greatest of all evils, but it's certainly near the top of the list. When war is far away and you read about it in a book or magazine, it may seem very glamorous; but when you're involved yourself or someone you love is involved, it's an entirely different story. War rips apart the unity of the human family. It liberates the darker impulses of the human spirit; and inevitably, it's the innocent who suffer most. War must be labeled a catastrophic human occurrence. Can it ever be justified? If so, under what conditions, and who decides? For the individual citizen, is it still 'Theirs not to reason why; theirs but to do and die'? Or in a democracy, must the individual citizen think it through for himself and make his own decision?

#199 Mr. Johnson's Had the Course

Producer: John Meredyth Lucas; Director: Leonard Horn; Writer: Stanford Whitmore

Cast: Robert Lansing, David Macklin, June Dayton, Kathy Garver, Pat Cardi, Bob Duggan

A failing college student holds the professor who failed him and his family at gunpoint. Love and hate collide as the professor tries to reach into the young man's pain.

David Macklin and Robert Lansing in Mr. Johnson's Had the Course

#200 The Sandalmaker

Producer: John Meredyth Lucas; Director: John Newland; Writer: David Moessinger

Cast: Brian Keith, Don Quine, Tim O'Connor, Maidie Norman, Jeanne Collins

An angry young dropout's girlfriend is murdered while both are on an LSD trip. His father, a lawyer, must decide if he can defend his accused son. Both are forced to rethink their lives and relationship.

#201 The 34th Hour

Producer: John Meredyth Lucas; Director: Marc Daniels; Writer: James Moser

Cast: Farley Granger, Guy Stockwell, Diana Muldaur, Edward Binns, Marian Moses, Irene Tsu, Walter Brooke

Six people and their therapist come together for an "encounter group" weekend, removing their masks and revealing their true feelings.

Guy Stockwell and Diana Muldaur in The 34th Hour

#202 The Ballad of Alma Gerlayne

Producer: John Meredyth Lucas; Director: Paul Stanley; Writer: Ed Waters

Cast: Sheilah Wells, Lou Antonio, Joseph Campanella, Edward Ashley, Don Chastain

A young and beautiful vocalist makes it to the top, attaining the money, men, and prestige she has always wanted. The search for meaning, however, goes on.

Lou Antonio and Sheilah Wells in The Ballad of Alma Gerlayne

#203 The Ghetto Trap

Producer: John Meredyth Lucas; Director: Hal Cooper; Writer: Maureen Daly

Cast: James Westerfield, Geoffrey Deuel, Virginia Gregg, William Bassett, Janet MacLachlan, D'urville Martin, John Dennis

A poor family is stuck in their destitute situation. They can't pay their bills, and the son fights with his father and quits school. Then a cousin arrives from Poland with the American dream.

Virginia Gregg and Geoffrey Deuel in The Ghetto Trap

#204 Watts Made Out of Thread

Producer: John Furia, Jr.; Director: Jack Shea; Writer: William Peter Blatty

Cast: Harold Gould, Roscoe Lee Browne, Alice Ghostley

A guilt-ridden ghetto exploiter who is burdened by the negative influence of his mother, decides to take his own life. While dying, he meets a black Christ.

66 • INSIGHT

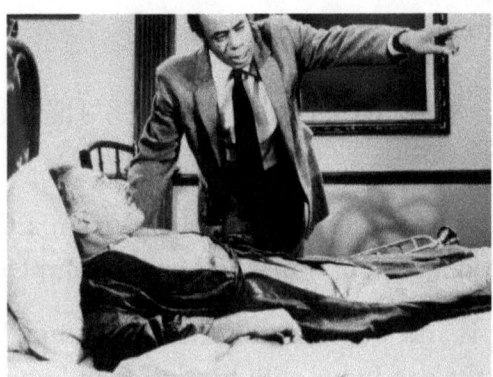

Harold Gould and Roscoe Lee Browne in Watts Made Out of Thread

Fr. Kieser's prologue to "Watts Made Out of Thread"

We have all sinned. Some more, some less grievously. That's what Seneca, the great Roman sage said. Unfortunately, sin is part of the human condition. I've abused my freedom; you have abused yours. And because we have, we feel guilty. Guilt is not a pleasant emotion, but it is a healthy one, for it's the natural consequence of sin. It's nature's way of saying to us: You're not acting in accordance with your dignity. You're not treating other people as you should. To feel guilt when you have not sinned is neurotic. But to feel guilt when you have sinned, is the sign of a spiritually and psychologically healthy person. But what do we do with guilt? How do we handle it? Do we try to turn it off? Do we try to escape from it by denying responsibility for what we've done? Or do we face up to the guilt, accepting the consequences of our actions? If we do, can sin be forgiven? Can guilt be assuaged?

#205 All the Things I've Never Liked

Producer: John Furia, Jr.; Director: Curt Conway; Writer: James M. Miller

Cast: Andrew Prine, Ellen McRae, Mark Roberts, Jeanne Bal, Elizabeth Baur, Esther Almaraz

A successful young dentist realizes he has built his whole life, including his marriage, on false values. He tries to explain this to his wife who admits to her own inauthenticity. Now they have to decide how to move forward.

#206 The Late Great God

Producer: John Furia, Jr.; Director: Harvey Hart; Writer: E. Sarsfield Waters

Cast: Ann B. Davis, Nancy Malone, Paul Carr, Antoinette Bower, Heather Young, Stanya Lowe, John Marley, Don Hammer, Richard Bull, Tony Zodrow

A teenage girl looking for love in life is drawn into a wild beach party where God is impeached. She hears stories of abuse and hypocrisy but hopes for something beyond the pain surrounding her.

Nancy Malone and Paul Carr in The Late Great God

1969

Fr. Kieser continued his central role in production, and credits began to refer to him as Executive Producer.

Episodes this year ran the gamut from Thomas Caramagno's poignant "Prince in the Apple Town," to Jack Hanrahan's metaphorical "The Poker Game;" from Robert Goodwin's literate "The Death of Simon Jackson," to Carol Sobieski's sci-fi fantasy "Sam."

James McGinn, who wrote fifteen shows for Paulist Productions over the years, premiered his first episode, "No Tears for Kelsey."

#307 No Tears for Kelsey

Producer: John Meredyth Lucas; Director: Hal Cooper; Writer: Jim McGinn

Cast: Lloyd Bochner, Geraldine Brooks, Deborah Winters, Don Mitchell

The generation gap has become an abyss in the home of fourteen-year-old Kathleen. She rebels against her uptight father and establishment mother by running away and embracing a hippie lifestyle.

Lloyd Bochner and Deborah Winters in No Tears for Kelsey

#308 Tuesday Night Is the Loneliest Night of the Week

Producer: John Meredyth Lucas; Director: Seymour Robbie; Writer: Maureen Daly

Cast: Louise Sorel, Joseph Campanella, Rosanna Huffman, Jonathan Lippe

The attractive editor of a woman's magazine finds she can really communicate with one of her co-workers, and she accepts his advances. The problem is, he's married.

#309 Prince in the Apple Town

Producer: John Meredyth Lucas; Director: Ralph Senensky; Writer: Thomas C. Caramagno

Cast: Jane Wyman, Gene Raymond

Two older, married actors perform their last play in a theatre that will be bulldozed to make way for a parking lot. They spend their last night reminiscing on the stage about the passions and griefs that accompanied them through life, and the possibility of more.

#310 The Poker Game

Producer: John Meredyth Lucas; Director: Ralph Senensky; Writer: Jack Hanrahan

Cast: Beau Bridges, Bill Bixby, Jeff Hunter, Peter Haskell, Ed Asner, Don Dubbins, Booker Bradshaw

Six old friends are joined by an uninvited stranger at their weekly poker game. The Christ-like figure's simple observations and questions trigger some destructive reactions and revelations.

> **Fr. Kieser's prologue to "The Poker Game"**
>
> It's sometimes difficult to face reality. Especially the reality about ourselves. Yet we die inside unless we do. Why are we so afraid to be ourselves? Because somehow or other we've gotten the idea that we're evil. We don't like what we feel we are. And so, we spend all kinds of time and energy running away. Different people do this in different ways. Some people refuse to feel. They exclude from consciousness any unpleasant emotion. Other people build false fronts to deceive other people and themselves. Still others have to constantly prove to themselves that they're not as bad as they think they are. The man who lives for money, who must have power, who feels the need to constantly demonstrate his sexual prowess is doing this. He's running away from himself. Are we really that bad? I don't think so. Sure, we all have problems. But with the time and energy we spend running away, we could easily solve those problems, and become the kinds of persons we want to be.

#311 *(Lost episode)*

#312 The Day God Died

Producer: John Meredyth Lucas; Director: Paul Stanley; Writer: James Moser

Cast: Efrem Zimbalist, Jr., Beverly Garland, Diana Muldaur, Tim O'Connor, Carroll O'Connor, Mariette Hartley, Roger Perry, Mark Lenard, Tina Menard, Ralph Manza, Lloyd Bochner

God is officially declared dead. After a university memorial service, faculty and regents meet for cocktails, while discussing who is responsible for the demise. Then, strange events start occurring.

Carroll O'Connor in The Day God Died

#313 A Thousand Red Flowers

Producer: John Meredyth Lucas; Director: Dan Petrie; Writer: John Bloch

Cast: Tony Bill, Robert Lipton, Brenda Scott, Barbara Hale, Bill Williams, Karl Swenson

A failing college sophomore kills himself. Afterwards, there is an imaginary trial involving his parents, girlfriend, and counselor to ascertain "Why?"

#314 The Death of Simon Jackson

Producer: John Meredyth Lucas; Director: Ralph Senensky; Writer: Robert Goodwin

Cast: Robert Doqui, Joel Fluellen, Judy Pace, Richard Elkins, Booker Bradshaw, Liam Dunn, Douglas Mitchell

A militant black poet tries to write the truth about his experience but can't get published. He finds himself caught between the proponents of violence and those who are fearful of confrontation.

Judy Pace and Joel Fluellen in The Death of Simon Jackson

#315 Charlie, You Made the Night Too Long

Producer: John Meredyth Lucas; Director: John Meredyth Lucas; Writer: William McGivern

Cast: Malachi Throne, Nancy Kovak, Henry Beckman, Linden Chiles, Hal Frederick, Bill Walker, Lea Weaver, Dilart Heyson, Ken Renard

Members of the white establishment are driving through a black ghetto when their car breaks down. They seek refuge in a local bar as a riot is about to break out.

Nancy Kovak and Bill Walker in Charlie, You Made the Night Too Long

Fr. Kieser's prologue to "Charlie, You Made the Night Too Long"

Racial polarization. Black and white forming separate communities, each cutting off meaningful contact with the other, sometimes actually warring on the other. It's a terrifying prospect: the unity of the nation disrupted, its energy sapped, its civic peace shattered. A tragedy of catastrophic proportions. The welfare of all of our citizens threatened. We've been warned, but have we heard? Have we grasped the reality and the seriousness of this situation? What are we doing about it? Isn't it possible that our existence as one nation under God is jeopardized because there hasn't been 'liberty and justice for all'? This is certainly the most serious issue of our generation. We all know there's a problem. But we tend to treat it as 'their' problem. Let somebody else solve it. It's 'our' problem. The bell tolls for all of us. What are you doing to purge your heart of any form of racism? Is the member of another race welcome in your neighborhood, in your home, at your dinner table? And what about your business, your labor union, your social club? Is the dignity of all respected, regardless of the pigment of their skin? Are they treated justly? And what are you doing to bridge the widening gap now separating the races? Have you tried to initiate meaningful dialogue? Have you taken steps to establish contact? Remember, the only thing it takes for the triumph of evil in the world is for good people to do nothing.

#316 Sam

Producer: John Meredyth Lucas; Director: Jack Shea; Writer: Carol Sobieski

Cast: Jack Albertson, Michael James Wixted, Joan Gerber

Computers have taken over the world. Only one human being, a vaudeville comedian, is left to search for love in an impersonal world.

#317 Is the 11:59 Late This Year?

Producer: John Meredyth Lucas; Director: Marc Daniels; Writer: Leon Tokatyan

Cast: Ann Southern, Howard Duff, Guy Stockwell, Roger C. Carmel, Marta Kristen, Hal Frederick, Alan Oppenheimer, Pitt Herbert, Joel Fluellen, Pauline Myers

Five desperate people who are running away from life wait frantically for a train that will take them away. They are joined by a mysterious "dispatcher" who hands them tickets. One of them, a flower child who has every reason to run away, reconsiders.

> "*Insight* was a remarkable and timely series. When I watch 'Is the 11:59 Late This Year?' I have the same response as when I see a play like 'Waiting for Godot.' The language is unique. It works on different levels that aren't easy to decipher. Who are these desperate, lost characters? Where are they going? What does it mean to choose hope?... It was a riveting, theatrical experience. I was young, and to be working with those highly skilled actors was something I've always kept in my heart."
>
> Marta Kristen

#318 Consider the Zebra

Producer: John Meredyth Lucas; Director: Buzz Kulik; Writer: John T. Dugan

Cast: Mario Alcalde, Lincoln Kilpatrick, Lynn Hamilton, Whit Bissell, Marion Ross, Val Devargas, Ed Begley

Urged on by an inner-city priest and nun, a parish council establishes a community center of black culture headed by a local black activist to reflect the changing demographics of the neighborhood. The council has second thoughts.

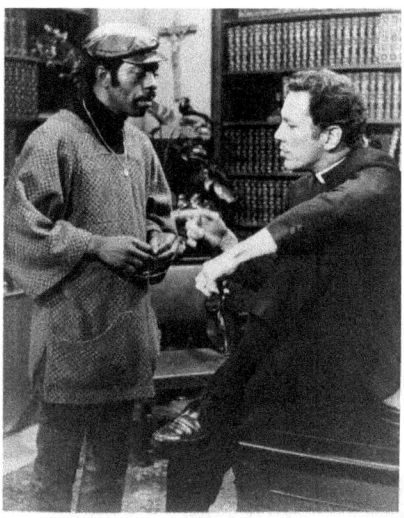

Lincoln Kilpatrick and Mario Alcalde in Consider the Zebra

1970

This year, Paulist Productions briefly experimented with offering free scripts of *Insight* episodes to its audience.

Intense psychological and social conflicts were explored in many episodes, including David Moessinger's "Incident on Danker Street," and E. Sarsfield Waters' "Hey, Hey, Billy Raye." Science fiction and fantasy continued to be represented in classics like William McGivern's "Dangerous Airs of Amy Clark," and Jack Hanrahan's "Old King Cole."

#319 The Seven Minute Life of James Houseworthy

Producer: John Furia, Jr.; Director: Ralph Senensky; Writer: John Zodrow

Cast: Edmund O'Brien, Bruce Davison, John Fielder, Christopher Cary, Jeanne Cooper, Lee Merriweather, Simon Scott, Steve Franken

The fawning relatives of a business tycoon gather around his casket for a reading of his will. He arises and confronts his nephew with the truth about the futile way he lived his life and how the young man is doing the same.

Edmund O'Brien and Bruce Davison in
The Seven Minute Life of James Houseworthy

#320 Incident on Danker Street

Producer: John Furia, Jr.; Director: Ted Post; Writer: David Moessinger

Cast: Beau Bridges. Andrew Duggan, Malachi Throne, Gail Fisher, Ken Lynch, Paul Bertoya, Hilly Hicks

A riot erupts between students and police. The mayor appoints a commission to investigate charges of police brutality. The investigation becomes a confrontation.

Fr. Kieser's prologue to "Incident on Danker Street"

Our society is dangerously fragmented. Blacks and whites, students and police, the young and the not so young, the haves and the have-nots, those who want to change society and those who like it pretty much the way it is. All too often they have turned each other off. They shout at each other, but they never really listen to each other. They are tempted to adopt an extreme position which allows no room for retreat, for compromise, for reasonable discussion—which allows really no consideration for the common good, for the welfare of all the people. Such a polarized situation is not healthy in any society. But fragmentation is particularly detrimental in a democratic one. For it works well only in an atmosphere of free and honest dialogue, where all segments of society are committed to the truth and to the common good, and where every opinion is given a respectful hearing, and can become national policy when it wins the support of most of the people. How do we promote such dialogue? How do both parties, once polarized, reestablish contact with each other? What, in short, is the remedy for fragmentation?

#321 Dangerous Airs of Amy Clark

Producer: John Furia, Jr.; Director: Hal Cooper; Writer: William McGivern

Cast: William Windom, Jane Wyatt, Haden Rorke, Chris Connolly, Heather Young, Karl Swenson, Paul Picerni, Roy Glenn, Ivor Francis, Nick Georgiade

The future earth is a polluted wasteland. In flashbacks, the president of a large corporation relives his role in the environmental disaster. Then the crisis becomes even more personal.

William Windom and Jane Wyatt in Dangerous Airs of Amy Clark

Fr. Kieser's prologue to "Dangerous Airs of Amy Clark"

When viewed from outer space, the earth looks like a beautiful green globe floating in a great sea of darkness. And when we walk over the world's surface and see its mountains and skies and oceans and plains and deserts, that perception is only reinforced. The world reflects the beauty of its creator. God's love made the world to support and nourish man's body and to uplift and enliven his spirit. But now all this is threatened. Air pollution, water pollution, contamination in all its myriad forms. Not only is the world's beauty threatened, but its very ability to sustain life. All of us agree this must not be allowed to happen. But how? Who's going to prevent it? The government? Industry? The consumer? Or each one of us? The ecologists say it will be very expensive. Who's going to pay for it? What price are you willing to pay for a clean environment? This is an economic and political question. But basically, it's a moral one. For God has given the earth to the whole human race, and its preservation and beauty is a responsibility of each one of us.

#322 Bourbon in Suburbia

Producer: John Furia, Jr.; Director: John Meredyth Lucas; Writer: John Meredyth Lucas

Cast: Anne Francis, Marie Windsor, Fred Beir, Paul Carr, Robert Doyle, Stefan Arngrim, Stan Schneider, Tani Phelps, Vincent Duke Milana

A Suburban housewife comes face to face with her alcoholism and its effect on the lives of her husband and children. Bewildered by her inability to cope with the problem, she reaches out for help.

Anne Francis in Bourbon in Suburbia

#323 Cry of Terror

Producer: John Furia, Jr.; Director: Ralph Senensky; Writer: Richard Alan Simmons

Cast: Mark Richman, Harry Townes, Andrew Prine, Al Checco, Vincent Duke Milana

A group of South American revolutionaries must decide whether or not to kill a hostage when one of their own members is executed by the reactionary government.

Mark Richman and Andrew Prine in Cry of Terror

#324 Old King Cole

Producer: John Furia, Jr.; Director: Ralph Senensky; Writer: Jack Hanrahan

Cast: Robert Emhardt, Martin Sheen, Steve Franken, Joyce Jameson, Nichelle Nichols, Billy Barty, Lisa Gerritsen

Mr. Cole lures a band of losers – a junkie poet, a fearful emcee, a faded husband and wife comedy team, and a stripper – into his bar. He promises to fulfill their dreams if they will abdicate their dignity and do his bidding. They agree, until a little blind girl, in love with life, wanders in.

Robert Emhardt, Martin Sheen, Steve Franken, Joyce Jameson, and Billy Barty in Old King Cole

#325 The Greatest Madness of Them All

Producer: John Furia, Jr.; Director: Paul Stanley; Writer: Tom Caramagno

Cast: John Marley, Jon Dehner, Brad David, Doreen Lang, Curt Lowens, Jennifer Leak, Jamie Hanrahan

A successful novelist is haunted by recurring nightmares. He travels through memories and his subconscious to face an abyss beyond himself. An intense chronicle of one man's search for personal wholeness.

John Marley and John Dehner in The Greatest Madness of Them All

Fr. Kieser's prologue to "The Greatest Madness of Them All"

It would be nice to be whole inside, all of one piece, interiorly unified. But that's just not the way things are. Deep within ourselves we find conflicting tendencies: between love and hate, hope and despair, reality and illusion. It almost seems that we're not one person. We're many people. And those many people within ourselves are afraid to face and communicate with each other; and so inside, we're fragmented. Like Humpty Dumpty, we've had a great fall. All the king's horses and all the king's men can't put Humpty Dumpty together again. Who can? Can we unify ourselves? Or must we go beyond ourselves for integration?

#326 Exit Sound

Producer: John Furia, Jr.; Director: Jack Shea; Writer: John Zodrow

Cast: Michael Burns, Tisha Sterling, Albert Brooks, Judy Kaye, Ford Rainey, William Wintersole, Dan Halleck, Maurice Warfield

An idealistic college senior despairs of changing the world. He joins a hippie commune and embraces the drug culture in search of peace and a community of love but finds neither.

#327 A Woman of Principle

Producer: John Furia, Jr.; Director: Richard Bennett; Writer: Leon Tokatyan

Cast: Audrey Totter, Nehemiah Persoff, Peter Duel, Ed Asner

An elderly widow is threatened with eviction when she can't pay her rent. She finally recognizes her need to reach out to others for support and kindness.

Peter Duel and Audrey Totter in A Woman of Principle

#328 Confrontation

Producer: John Furia, Jr.; Director: Arthur Hiller; Writer: John T. Dugan

Cast: Gene Hackman, Carl Betz, Earl Holliman, Ed Binns, Brandon de Wilde, Leonard Stone, Alan Oppenheimer

A priest, social worker, and college dissenter are convinced the Vietnam war is immoral. To register their protest, they defy the law and burn draft files. In court, they try to defend their actions.

Ed Binns, Carl Betz, and Gene Hackman in Confrontation

#329 Hey, Hey, Billy Raye

Producer: John Furia, Jr.; Director: Richard Bennett; Writer: E. Sarsfield Waters

Cast: Michael Burns, Jeff Bridges, Marj Redmond, Marion Ross, Noah Keen, Than Wyenn, Maura Bennett

A hero of the Vietnam war feels guilt over killing innocent Vietnamese women and children. He finds that neither the demands of war nor military authority absolves a person of responsibility for one's actions.

Michael Burns in Hey, Hey, Billy Raye

"[Insight] was filmed, but it was more theatre. Not live, but it felt like it was live... It was an honor to be on one of those shows. Those were good scripts. This isn't cheap stuff. It meant something."

Marion Ross

#330 *(Lost episode)*

1971

Modest production values never limited *Insight's* dramatic impact. This can certainly be seen in Michael Crichton's "War of the Eggs," an intense inquiry into physical child abuse.

Several scripts this year turned towards characters' inner life, including John and David Zodrow's "Ride a Turquois Pony," Leon Tokatyan's "The Highest Bidder," and John Meredyth Lucas' "The Bird on the Mast."

#331 The Death of Superman

Producer: John Meredyth Lucas; Director: Richard Bennett; Writer: John Zodrow

Cast: Britt Leach, Lane Bradbury, Tony Costello, Lurene Tuttle, Arlene Golonka, Frank Maxwell, Allan Lurie, Sallie Shockley

A simple-minded good Samaritan wants only to help people but is met with derision and ridicule because of his childlike ways.

#332 Crunch on Spruce Street

Producer: John Meredyth Lucas; Director: Hal Cooper; Writer: William McGivern

Cast: Harvey Korman, Joyce Van Patten, Tim Matheson, Paul Picerni, James McEachin, Ron Masak, George Lindsay

A proud hard-working man fears his way of life is threatened when he learns that a black family wants to buy a home in his neighborhood. At the same time, his son tells him he wants to leave the neighborhood for a place of his own.

Harvey Korman in Crunch on Spruce Street

"My agent called me and said, there's this show, *Insight*... They were written by the best people. The writers were great, the directors were great, and so I just said, selfishly, I can get exposed to these guys. I can learn from these people. I mean Harvey Korman was an amazing, brilliant comedian...but the precision with the way he worked as a dramatic actor...

"It was a spiritual show in the sense that it was about ethics, it was about morality, and it was about what makes people good."

Tim Matheson

#333 A Prayer from the Abyss

Producer: John Meredyth Lucas; Director: James Sheldon; Writer: Tom Caramagno

Cast: Bruce Davison, Patricia Barry, Tim O'Connor, Laurie Prange, Michael Fox

A girl trying to escape the harsh cruelties of the world attempts suicide and fails. A young psychiatric intern tries to help her on the long return to reality.

#334 The Wrinkle Squad

Producer: John Meredyth Lucas; Director: John Newland; Writer: Tom Caramagno

Cast: John Marley, Ed Asner, Edward Andrews, Kaz Garas, Barry Atwater, Bert Freed, Clint Howard

Three old men run afoul of the state bureaucracy when they open a child-care center as a way of halting the feeling of uselessness that accompanies old age. They find themselves in court pleading for their right to love life.

Bert Freed and John Marley in The Wrinkle Squad

#335 Ride A Turquoise Pony

Producer: John Meredyth Lucas; Director: Hal Cooper; Writer: John Zodrow, David Zodrow

Cast: Belinda Montgomery, Peter Duryea, Ralph Moody, Jan Clayton, Anne Seymour, John Larch, Eileen Baral

Reunited lovers find that two years of separation, the boy in Vietnam and the girl as a Vista volunteer at a Navajo reservation, have taken a toll. They've grown older and far apart.

John Larch and Belinda Montgomery in Ride a Turquoise Pony

> **Fr. Kieser's prologue to "Ride a Turquoise Pony"**
>
> Is God a stern old tyrant with darting eyes who's looking for an excuse to send us to hell? Is he a celestial Santa Clause that lives up in the clouds, has a long white beard, pats us on the head and gives us candy canes when we're good little boys? Or is God the loving ground of our being, who lives in us and yet flows beyond us; Someone who is seeking a loving, personal relationship with us? And where is God to be found? In outer space, beyond the stars? Or, in ourselves and in those around us? And how is God to be found? By sealing ourselves off from the world? Or by involving ourselves in that world, reaching out in love to our fellow human beings?

#336 The War of The Eggs

Producer: John Meredyth Lucas; Director: Lamont Johnson; Writer: Michael Crichton

Cast: Elizabeth Ashley, Bill Bixby, James Olson, Robert Rhodes, Stan Schneider

A heart wrenching drama plays out in a hospital waiting room. Despite material success, a young couple find themselves unhappy with each other, and vent their hostilities on their two-year-old son.

Bill Bixby and Elizabeth Ashley in The War of the Eggs

#337 No More Mañanas

Producer: John Meredyth Lucas; Director: Herb Kenwith; Writer: John Figueroa

Cast: Rafael Campos, Natividad Vacio, Frank Ramirez, Edith Diaz, Don Dubbins, Ron Trujillo, Bob Padilla, David Renard, Roberto Contreras

The director of a barrio self-help agency tries to convince a recently paroled addict to return some stolen money. If he doesn't, he risks police intervention, another prison term, and self-destruction.

#338 Five Without Faces

Producer: John Meredyth Lucas; Director: Nicholas Webster; Writer: Tom Caramagno

Cast: Tom Nardini, Michael Brandon, Gary Burghoff, Brian Avery, Carl Betz, Dan Ferrone, Harry Page

An American combat unit in Vietnam is ordered into a certain death situation in an attempt to cover up a My Lai-type atrocity and to bait the enemy.

#339 The Party

Producer: John Meredyth Lucas; Director: Nicholas Webster; Writer: Dave Moessinger, E. Sarsfield Waters

Cast: Pamela McMyler, Michael Burns, Bill Mumy, Joy Bang, Meredith Baxter, Michael Shea

During a weekend party, a teenage girl is torn by peer group pressure, the demands of her boyfriend, and her own feelings toward love and sexual commitment.

Michael Burns and Pamela McMyler in The Party

> From Fr. Kieser's prologue to "The Party"
>
> Authentic religion can only affirm the beauty of human sexuality. Afterall, it is God-given. It's part of the human personality. We can approach God through it. And we cannot grow to full human maturity without dealing with it. And any authentic appreciation of human sexuality must also recognize its limitations. Sex can take us toward perfect fulfillment. But it cannot deliver it. Only

> God can do that. The sexual act is a unique and privileged symbol between two human beings. To be honest, they must mean what that act says. What is that? What is required before the sexual act becomes honest?

#340 The Highest Bidder

Producer: John Meredyth Lucas; Director: John Meredyth Lucas; Writer: Leon Tokatyan

Cast: Howard Duff, Ida Lupino, Don Grady, Jack Albertson

Death shows up for a weekly bridge game in the guise of a mysterious stranger. He insists on being the host's bridge partner, and then unsettles people with his strange questions and observations.

Jack Albertson, Howard Duff, and Don Grady in The Highest Bidder

#341 The Bird on the Mast

Producer: John Meredyth Lucas; Director: Richard Bennett; Writer: John Meredyth Lucas

Cast: Tony Costello, Cecily Tyson, Greg Mullavey, Glynn Turman, Patricia Stich, Celeste Yarnell, Chic Casey, Alan Lurie

A young executive has tried unsuccessfully to escape his trapped and unhappy life through hallucinatory drugs and attempted suicide. Finally, he finds the inner freedom he was seeking in meditation.

Cicely Tyson on the set of The Bird on the Mast

1972

This year, Paulist Productions began advertising the availability of *Insight* episodes on 16mm film for distribution to schools and community groups.

Comedy writer Lan O'Kun's "A Box for Mr. Lipton" was the first of his 26 scripts to be produced by Paulist Productions.

Dramatic highlights from this year include: Jack Hanrahan's study of family grief in "Death of the Elephant," Edmund T. North's treatment of American foreign policy during the Cold War in "Nobody Loves a Rich Uncle," and Michael Crichton's takedown of celebrity culture and psychological defenses in "The Killer."

#342 A Box for Mr. Lipton

Producer: John Furia, Jr.; Director: Marc Daniels; Writer: Lan O'Kun

Cast: Ken Mars, Pat Barry, Robert Harris, Anne Seymour, David Bailey, Patty Mattick, Peggy Rae

When life becomes too much, Ben Lipton escapes into a large cardboard box in his back yard. He discovers that dealing with the craziness of life requires more than dropping out.

Ken Mars, Patricia Barry, and Anne Seymour in A Box for Mr. Lipton

#343 The Freak

Producer: John Furia, Jr.; Director: Paul Stanley; Writer: John Zodrow

Cast: Ed Asner, Tim Matheson, Jacqueline Scott, Hilarie Thompson

A father explodes when his "Jesus freak" son installs a telephone lifeline in his room for lonely, runaway kids. Then he discovers his only daughter is also a runaway.

Tim Matheson and Ed Asner in The Freak

#344 Why Don't you Call Me Skipper Anymore

Producer: John Furia, Jr.; Director: Richard Bennett; Writer: William McGivern

Cast: Robert Lansing, Beverley Garland, Davey Davison, Bill Christopher, Simon Scott

When a 21-year-old college graduate refuses to take a job that is not meaningful to her, she and her father clash over what it means to have a work ethic and to be a success.

#345 Death of the Elephant

Producer: John Furia, Jr.; Director: Richard Bennett; Writer: Jack Hanrahan

Cast: Ford Rainey, John Astin, Martin Sheen, Maggie Malooly, Diane Baker

An Irish wake for their larger-than-life father triggers some strong and deep self-revelations among four very different siblings.

John Astin and Diane Baker in Death of the Elephant

Fr. Kieser's prologue to "Death of the Elephant"

Some mothers and fathers are good and loving and gracious. And others are hung up, frightened and tyrannical. And most are somewhere in between. But whether good or bad or in between, they're ours. We're part of them, they're part of us. There's no getting away from that. Nor is there any denying the extent of their influence upon us. They shape our whole approach to life. They mold our psyches; they influence our values. Whether dead or alive they continue to live within us, which means we have to learn to deal with them. If we expect them to be perfect like God, we're certainly going to be disappointed, and we'll probably end up fighting with them and blaming them for our shortcomings. If, on the other hand, we accept them for what they are, fallible human beings like ourselves, then we'll be able to enter into a loving relationship with them, and go on to live our own, independent lives.

#346 Nobody Loves a Rich Uncle

Producer: John Meredyth Lucas; Director: Paul Stanley; Writer: Edmund H. North

Cast: Carl Betz, Michael Burns, Booker T. Bradshaw Jr., Dennis Robertson

A presidential envoy lands in a South Asian country to conduct delicate negotiations. His son is a Peace Corps volunteer in the same country, and they clash over what kind of aid the U.S. should be giving.

#347 Love Song of the Coo Coo Birds

Producer: John Meredyth Lucas; Director: Hal Cooper; Writer: Carol Sobieski

Cast: Jonathan Harris, Florence Halop, Karen Jensen

A young social worker is assigned to the care and rehab of two disabled senior citizens. Much to her consternation, the cantankerous and wacky elderly couple fall in love.

Florence Halop and Johnathan Harris in Love Song of the Coo Coo Birds

#348 The System

Producer: John Furia, Jr.; Director: Ralph Senensky; Writer: Lan O'Kun

Cast: Richard Jaeckel, Arlene Golonka, McLean Stevenson, Harvey Lembeck

Mary likes to live dangerously and have fun. Henry plays by the rules and doesn't take chances. Circumstances cause them to learn from each other.

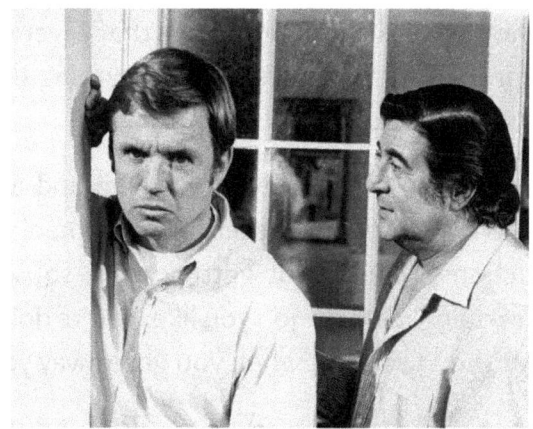

Richard Jaeckel and Harvey Lembeck in The System

#349 The Killer

Producer: John Furia, Jr.; Director: Robert Butler; Writer: Michael Crichton

Cast: Alex Cord, Joe Flynn, Joyce Bulifant, Ivor Francis, Sandy Kenyon, Frances Spanier

Sex Symbol Tom Slade comes apart when grilled on a TV talk show. Will he face the unresolved rage within himself or continue to play a role?

Joe Flynn, Alex Cord, Ivor Francis, and Joyce Bulifant in The Killer

> "[Fr. Kieser] was one of the best producers that I ever worked for... meticulously producing and overseeing everything that went on. Tough, good, strong producer...
>
> "It was he who threw a net over me, smiled and asked for his money back... We all signed our check over immediately back to Paulist Productions... You're not getting paid, so what are you doing?... You're doing it for the job you like. You're doing what you want to do. And you proved it when you gave away your money!"
>
> Robert Butler, Director

#350 *(Lost episode)*

#351 **Friends**

Producer: John Furia, Jr.; Director: Richard Bennett; Writer: Lan O'Kun

Cast: Amzie Strickland, Woodrow Parfrey, Frank Aletter, Marlyn Mason, Bill Quinn

For twenty years, a kind-hearted lady has lovingly cared for a mentally disabled man. Stricken with a heart attack, she must now find someone else to care for him.

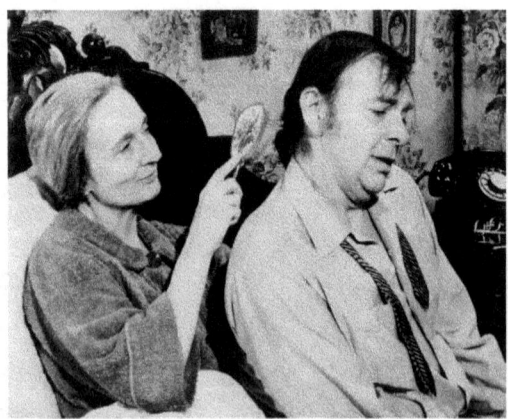

Amzie Strickland and Woodrow Parfrey in Friends

#352 *(Lost episode)*

#353 **I'm Gonna Be Free**

Producer: John Meredyth Lucas; Director: Richard Bennett; Writer: Harvey Lerner, David Moessinger

Cast: Kaz Garas, Diana Muldaur, John Larch, Walter Brooke, Barry Cahill, James McEachin

At a parole board hearing, an inmate explodes in rage at himself and at the prison system. He argues for reform and release. The board must decide if he is ready or if they are being conned.

Kaz Garas in I'm Gonna Be Free

#354 **Graduation Day**

Producer: John Meredyth Lucas; Director: John Meredyth Lucas; Writer: James McGinn

Cast: Gary Collins, Skye Aubrey, Joyce Van Patten, Francis Spanier, Noah Keen, Bernie Kopell, Dennis Burkley, Robert Reiser

An eighteen-year-old delinquent who pops pills, sleeps around, and attempts suicide can no longer stay in the juvenile court system. What she has going for her is a probation officer who actually cares.

Garry Collins in Graduation Day

#355 The Jesus Song

Producer: John Meredyth Lucas; Director: Jack Shea; Writer: Jack Hanrahan

Cast: Bruce Davison, Pam McMyler, Bob Doqui, Alan Oppenheimer, Cynthia Hull, Peter Leeds

The career of a folk-rock singer peaks, then bottoms out. When he meets a mysterious handyman who becomes a collaborator, he begins to relearn where his creativity comes from.

Bruce Davison in The Jesus Song

1973

This year, a new opening animation for the show premiered, with a change in introduction: "*Insight*: Stories of modern man's search for meaning, freedom, love." New concluding words were introduced over the final credits: "*Insight* is a production of the Paulist Fathers, a group of Catholic priests who seek to share the good news of God's love with all their brothers and sisters in the human family."

#356 Roommates on a Rainy Day

Producer: John Meredyth Lucas; Director: Paul Stanley; Writer: James McGinn

Cast: Martin Sheen, Pamela Murphy, Jim Antonio, Dick Van Patten, Hilarie Thompson

Jenny and Vince are "roommates." He likes the arrangement. She wants more, namely marriage. They explore the meaning of commitment in a world of other possibilities.

#357 Reunion

Producer: John Meredyth Lucas; Director: Charles S. Dubin; Writer: William McGivern

Cast: Ron Rifkin, Don Stroud, Ron Glass, Robert Foxworth, Murray Macleod, Felice Orlandi

A wild and boisterous high school reunion turns sour when a masked killer intrudes. A group of old friends must decide if they have the courage to help their friend who is the target.

#358 Happy Birthday, Marvin

Producer: John Meredyth Lucas; Director: Hal Cooper; Writer: Lan O'Kun

Cast: Bob Newhart, Anne Francis, Harold Gould, Clint Howard, Ivor Francis

Marvin is going to be 40 and isn't handling it well. He's convinced he's going to die on his birthday. A comic encounter with the crisis of middle age.

Bob Newhart and Anne Francis in Happy Birthday, Marvin

"Father Kieser asked me to do an *Insight* episode, so I thought it was going to be a very Catholic operation. Then I discovered the writer was Jewish. The director was Jewish. The other actors were Jewish. They aren't the chosen people for nothing. But I couldn't figure out how I fit in. Then I realized the part called for a nebbish, and there was no Jewish one available."[7]

Bob Newhart

#359 Truck Stop

Producer: John Meredyth Lucas; Director: Marc Daniels; Writer: Lan O'Kun

Cast: Tim Matheson, Deborah Winters, John Astin, Pat Barry, Marshall Reed

A tough young waitress goes from man to man in her search for sexual identity, until she is brought face to face with her own need for roots and emotional security.

#360 Attention Must Be Paid

Producer: John Meredyth Lucas; Director: Paul Stanley; Writer: Lan O'Kun

Cast: Ned Glass, Leon Belasco, George Tobias, Amzie Strickland, Oscar Beregi, Peter Brocco

A group of senior citizens in an assisted living home find new meaning and hope in their lives as, one by one, they are drawn into the loving world of one of the cancer-stricken residents.

Ned Glass in Attention Must Be Paid

#361 Bloodstrike

Producer: John Meredyth Lucas; Director: John Meredyth Lucas; Writer: David Moessinger

Cast: Michael Learned, Tom Nardini, James McMullan, Frank Aletter, Walter Brooke, Joel Fluellen, Henry Proach, Tim Bloch

Sr. Janet instills new pride into a group of derelicts and leads them in a protest against the dehumanizing practices of the local plasma bank.

> Fr. Kieser's Prologue to "Bloodstrike":
>
> What does it mean to believe? It means to allow yourself to be grasped by God. It means to surrender yourself to the loving ground of your being and to allow him to take over in your life. Jesus was this kind of man. He was transparent to the light and life of his Father. He was so filled with the Father's love that he reached out to enrich all those around him. He was brother, friend, and servant to everyone he met. But he did have a special preference for the poor and the sinful, the exploited and rejected. He freely gravitated toward them. Why? Because they needed him most. He felt their pain. He ministered to their needs. He fought for their rights. He identified himself with them. Jesus did this, but how about us? Can we do what he did, at least to some extent, on our own or with his help? And what happens to us, inside I mean, when we try?

#362 The Resurrection of Joe Hammond

Producer: John Meredyth Lucas; Director: Richard Bennett; Writer: Jack Hanrahan

Cast: Clu Gulager, Nita Talbot, Anthony Costello, Sharon Dierking, Allan Lurie, Peggy Doyle, Diane Shalet, Jonathan Lippe, Art Metrano, Robert Duggan, Romarie Hanrahan, Laurie Prange

In a psychiatric hospital, a man discovers he has no monopoly on human frailty. After a nervous breakdown, he begins the long road back to mental health.

Clu Gulager and Anthony Costello in The Resurrection of Joe Hammond

#363 The Coming of The Clone

Producer: John Meredyth Lucas; Director: Murray Golden; Writer: John T. Dugan

Cast: Gary Collins, Brooke Bundy, Ed Andrews, Sandra Gould, Barry Sullivan,

A scientist announces to his wife that they are having a baby, but not in the usual way. She will be the first mother of a genetically manipulated clone. Now they have to convince an outstanding human specimen to be the father.

#364 Eye of The Camel

Producer: John Meredyth Lucas; Director: John Meredyth Lucas; Writer: William McGivern

Cast: Gregory Sierra, Nehemiah Persoff, Henry Darrow, Roberto Contreras, Val de Vargas, A Martinez, Henry Proach

A South American bishop finds himself caught between the local capitalists and a radical young priest trying to form a union for the workers. When things turn violent, the bishop is forced to choose sides.

> **Fr. Kieser's prologue to "Eye of the Camel"**
>
> The Church is people. But what are they about? What's the purpose of the Church? To celebrate God's presence among his people? To share God's love with those who do not as yet enjoy it? To help all to grow and develop and discover the meaning of their lives? To expand their consciousness, deepen their freedom, experience their oneness with all others? To construct a humane society where justice and love prevail, and the rights and dignity of all are recognized? Yes, what is the purpose of the Church?

#365 Hey, Janitor

Producer: John Meredyth Lucas; Director: Richard Bennett; Writer: Jim Moser

Cast: Robert Foxworth, Gregory Sierra, Robert Mandan, Lara Parker, Peggy Doyle, Donnelly Rhodes, Ginny Golden, Kitty Carl, Misty Rowe

An up-and-coming young executive idolizes and imitates his power-driven boss. But when the boss, empty and despairing, kills himself, the young man's world comes apart. A mysterious custodian shows him how to rebuild it.

#366 Celebration in Fresh Powder

Producer: John Meredyth Lucas; Director: Paul Stanley; Writer: E. Sarsfield Waters

Cast: Candace Clark, Joan Prather, Lynne Marta, Shari Bernath, Rick Kelman, Michael Shea

On a ski weekend, Ginny shocks three of her high school classmates by announcing she's pregnant. As the weekend progresses, she struggles with her options.

Candace Clark and Rick Kelman in Celebration in Fresh Powder

1974

A number of performances stood out this year, such as: John Astin and Patty Duke Astin in Lan O'Kun's "The One-Armed Man;" Larry

Pressman and Sharon Farrell in Michael Crichton's "The Theft;" and Martin Sheen in Terry Sweeney's "The Clown of Freedom."

Terry Sweeney's "The Clown of Freedom" was the first *Insight* episode to be shot entirely outside of a studio.

#367 Eddie

Producer: John Meredyth Lucas; Director: Paul Stanley; Writer: Jim McGinn

Cast: Don Stroud, Ellen Geer, Barney Phillips, Norman Cole, Art Metrano, Laurence Haddon, Elizabeth Lucas

A young working-class couple must come to grips with their feelings when their first child is born with Down's Syndrome.

Don Stroud in Eddie

#368 The Crime of Innocence

Producer: John Meredyth Lucas; Director: Marc Daniels; Writer: David Moessinger

Cast: Martin Sheen, Lynn Carlin, Elliott Street, Craig Hundley, Alan Oppenheimer, John Lupton, Johana de Winter, Paul Sorensen

A neighborhood becomes frightened when a houseful of mentally disabled teenagers and their director move in. The Homeowners Association fights to remove them from the community, while the director argues passionately for their inclusion.

Martin Sheen in The Crime of Innocence

#369 And the Walls Came Tumbling Down

Producer: John Meredyth Lucas; Director: Richard Bennett; Writer: Lan O'Kun

Cast: Jack Albertson, Martin Sheen, Angela Clarke, Ty Wilson

God decides to reveal himself to an aging tailor between heartbeats. The result is a new appreciation for life and a greater capacity for doing good.

Martin Sheen and Jack Albertson in And the Walls Came Tumbling Down

#370 The One-Armed Man

Producer: John Meredyth Lucas; Director: Seymour Robbie; Writer: Lan O'Kun

Cast: John Astin, Patty Duke Astin, Diane Shalet, Henry Proach, Michael Strong, Beau Gibson, Mary Robin Redd, Jon King, Todd Gross, Moira Albertson, Martha Aniano, Bennie Dobbins, Bob Duggan

A one-armed man struggles with loneliness; but the possibility for a relationship tears away at his false self-sufficiency and pretensions.

John Astin and Patty Duke in The One-Armed Man

#371 The Theft

Producer: John Meredyth Lucas; Director: Arthur Hiller; Writer: Michael Crichton

Cast: Larry Pressman, Sharon Farrell, Lou Antonio

An armed burglar finds himself drawn in as a referee in the on-going battle of a young suburban couple with serious communication issues.

Sharon Farrell and Lawrence Pressman in The Theft

Fr. Kieser's prologue to "The Theft"

In a healthy marriage, husband and a wife stand opposite each other, open to each other, saying yes to each other. They stand opposite each other because each is a separate person, a world unto themselves, good in themselves. Neither is a satellite of the other. Each is responsible to himself for himself. They stand open to each other because they've freely decided and chosen to share themselves with the other. They do this by allowing themselves to be known, not as they would like to be but as they actually are, in all their naked vulnerability and frightening ambivalence. They say yes to the other, not because he's a genial conversationalist, a good provider, or a strong shoulder in time of need. Not because she's a gracious hostess, an exciting partner in bed, or a good mother. No, each says yes to the other not for what he or she does, but rather for what he or she is: a human person etched in the image and likeness of God. This is what the marital relationship can be, but sometimes getting there is a long and arduous process.

#372 When You See Arcturus

Producer: John Meredyth Lucas; Director: Marc Daniels; Writer: James E. Moser

Cast: Efrem Zimbalist Jr., William Windom, Christine Belford, Mark Hamill, Jack Manning, Peg Porter, Alan Dexter

A man is so bored with existence that he hires the director of "The Thanatos," a society that aids people's suicides, to assist him in ending his life. But first he wants to meet with the daughter and son he left behind long ago.

#373 The Man Who Went Blue Sky

Producer: John Meredyth Lucas; Director: Ralph Senensky; Writer: Lan O'Kun

Cast: Wendell Burton, Kristina Holland, Elliott Street, Woodrow Parfrey, Arlen Stuart, Bill Quinn, Jack Manning, Olan Soule

A man invents beautiful things, none of which are practical. He comes to realize that his genius will survive when it stops trying to fit into a programmed and practical society and remains free.

Kristina Holland and Wendell Burton in The Man Who Went Blue Sky

#374 The Clown of Freedom

Producer: John Meredyth Lucas; Director: John Meredyth Lucas; Writer: Terry Sweeney

Cast: Martin Sheen, Alan Oppenheimer, Gary Morgan, Richmond Shepard, Joseph McCord, Anthony Costello, Henry Proach, Bill Quinn, Bob Hyman, Sander Johnson

Bobo and his street theatre troupe are arrested by a military junta in Latin America for being hostile to the regime. Bobo is sentenced to a firing squad, and his execution becomes his final performance.

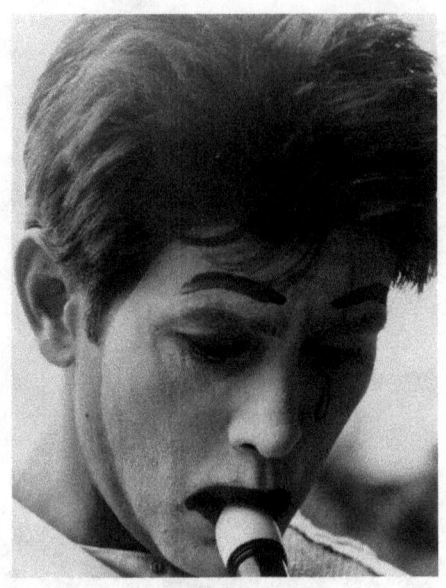

Martin Sheen in The Clown of Freedom

> "['Clown of Freedom'] was grounded in my experience in travelling through Salvador at the time the guerilla warfare was going on... I wrote it as part of a master's thesis I was doing at Loyola Marymount University and I had the help of a director by the name of Byron Haskin who did *The War of the Worlds,* and he helped me in the dramatic structuring of this *Insight* script. He appreciated that I had the experience of being in Salvador... I was very proud of it."
>
> Terry Sweeney, Writer

#375 Mohawk

Producer: John Meredyth Lucas; Director: Richard Bennett; Writer: Howard Fast, as E.V. Cunningham

Cast: Richard Yniguez, Robert Hogan, Frank Aletter, Andrew Duggan, Michael Richardson, Peggy Doyle

A Native American man decides to sit in front of the doors of a cathedral to meditate. A policeman threatens to arrest him for disturbing the peace, a priest engages him in a theological conversation, and the media tries to question him.

Richard Yniguez and Robert Hogan in Mohawk

#376 *(Lost episode)*

#377 King of the Penny Arcade

Producer: Ellwood Kieser; Director: Richard Bennett; Writer: Michael Alan Humm

Cast: Mitch Vogel, Lee Purcell, Ed Begley Jr., Rick Kelman, Vic Tayback, Davey Davison, Mike Pataki, Lance Kerwin, Janis Lynn, David Bailey

An eighteen-year-old is a drunk and is wasting his life. After a night with false friends, he knows he needs help.

> "Fr. Kieser was a very amiable fellow. I liked him right away... On *Insight* we weren't lax about the schedule, but it was more relaxed than the other shows, and a very pleasant set to be on. All good memories..."
>
> Ed Begley, Jr.

1975

This year gave us some exceptional examples of the use of fantasy in exploration of spiritual themes: John T. Duggan's "The Placement Service;" William Peter Blatty's "The Man from Inner Space;" John Zodrow's "All Out;" and Lan O'Kun's "Somewhere Before."

Performances that deserve mention include: John Astin and Cliff DeYoung in Terry Sweeney's "Out of the Depths;" Kim Hunter in James McGinn's "Last of the Great Male Chauvinists;" and James McEachin's tour de force in J.S. Sugerhill's "Hellbound Blues."

The episode "Last of the Great Male Chauvinists" may be the earliest to grapple directly with social critiques from the women's movement of that time.

#378 The Prodigal Father

Producer: John Meredyth Lucas; Director: Marc Daniels; Writer: Terry Sweeney

Cast: Biff McGuire, Eileen Brennan, Jim McMullan, Debralee Scott, Henry Proach, Marguerite Ray, Loren James

After years of separation, a young man faces his alcoholic and compulsive gambling father, as well as his own inability to forgive.

Jim McMullan and Biff McGuire in The Prodigal Father.

#379 The Placement Service

Producer: John Meredyth Lucas; Director: Paul Stanley; Writer: John T. Dugan

Cast: Jack Carter, Edward Andrews, James McEachin, Edith Diaz, Nancy McCormick,

Two men, a successful businessman and a flawed entertainer, find themselves reviewing their lives for the "final placement"—eternity.

Edward Andrews in The Placement Service

> Fr. Kieser's prologue to "The Placement Service"
>
> All of us on occasion cop out, abdicate our dignity, and violate the rights of those around us. Which is just another way of saying that we're all sinners. Now there are just two ways of handling this fundamental fact of the human experience. One way is by honestly facing up to it, admitting our weakness to ourselves and to those around us. The other way is to deny it. How do you handle it?

#380 Chipper

Producer: John Meredyth Lucas; Director: Richard Bennett; Writer: Lan O'Kun

Cast: Martin Sheen, John McMartin, Diane Shalet

A man drops by to visit his old buddy who owns a restaurant but is met by a strange waiter who seems to know a lot about him. The waiter is there to serve in more ways than one.

John McMartin and Martin Sheen in Chipper

#381 Somewhere Before

Producer: John Meredyth Lucas; Director: Paul Stanley; Writer: Lan O'Kun

Cast: Mariette Hartley, Ron Howard, Cindy Williams, Pamela Franklin, Bob Hogan, Jack Manning, David Bailey, Peggy Doyle

An unmarried girl about to give birth cannot decide if life is truly worth living. Meanwhile, the life of her child waits in the wings to be born.

Ron Howard and Pamela Franklin in Somewhere Before

#382 The Incredible Man

Producer: John Meredyth Lucas; Director: Richard Bennett; Writer: Lan O'Kun

Cast: John David Carson, Tom Bosley, Gary Burghoff, Ed Begley Jr., Victor Tayback, Ty Henderson, Trish Soodik

A star-struck high school basketball player lives in a fantasy world. That world is shattered when he visits his favorite comic book hero, the Incredible Man.

John David Carson, Gary Burghoff, and Victor Tayback in The Incredible Man

#383 Welcome Home

Producer: John Meredyth Lucas; Director: Ralph Senensky; Writer: Lydia Wiggins

Cast: Jerry Houser, Dick Van Patten, Robert Hogan, Lindsey Jones, Nan Martin, John Mark Robinson, Oscar DeGruy, Jr.

Returning from juvenile detention camp, a teenage boy is welcomed home by his domineering mother and ineffective father. With the help of a Probation Officer, he begins to find a connection with his dad.

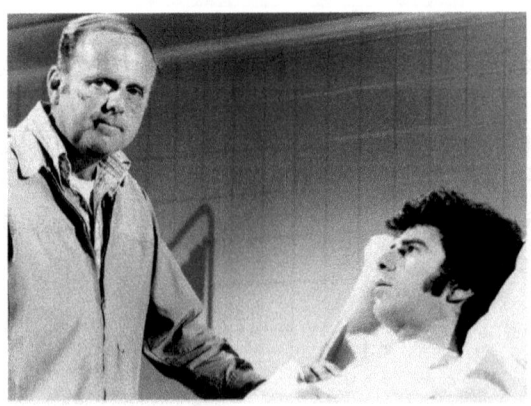

Dick Van Patten and Jerry Hauser in Welcome Home

#384 Hunger Knows My Name

Producer: John Meredyth Lucas; Director: James Sheldon; Writer: William McGivern

Cast: William Daniels, Lynn Carlin, Sam Chew, Janet MacLachlan, Joan Prather, Richard Beymer, Richard O'Neill, Tim Matheson, Dorothy Meyer

An affluent American family becomes bitter when they discover their only son has died while working on a famine prevention program in Nigeria. Then, they discover the impact their son had.

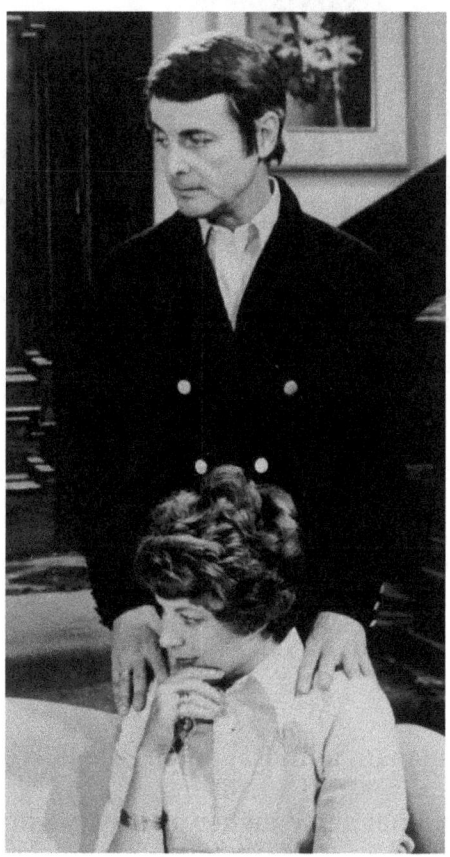

William Daniels and Lynn Carlin in Hunger Knows My Name

#385 Last of the Great Male Chauvinists

Producer: John Meredyth Lucas; Director: Richard Bennett; Writer: James McGinn

Cast: Kim Hunter, Don Porter, Patricia Barry, Ramon Bieri, Kristina Holland, Jerry Houser

A middle-aged woman, her family now grown, is feeling left out and useless. After her husband's heart attack, she changes her life's direction.

Kim Hunter and Don Porter in Last of the Great Male Chauvinists

#386 Seventeen Forever

Producer: John Meredyth Lucas; Director: Hal Cooper; Writer: David Vowell

Cast: Rue McClanahan, John Randolph, Lee Purcell

A grandfather, mother and daughter are all caught up in preserving their youth. Each in their own way is trying to figure out who they are at this stage of their lives.

Lee Purcell and Rue McClanahan in Seventeen Forever

"There is such a thing as acting for a higher purpose... *Insight* was an anomaly. It was very unusual. How did it exist? Because of Fr. Kieser... He was very much present and very much involved. He didn't just hire you and go away. He was on the set the whole time. He was encouraging and insightful."

Lee Purcell

#387 The Man from Inner Space

Producer: John Meredyth Lucas; Director: Richard Bennett; Writer: William Peter Blatty

Cast: Lou Gossett, James Franciscus, Frank Aletter

Hundreds of people watch a black man emerge from a spaceship. He works wonders and teaches about love and trust. He asks to talk to the President of the United States but is whisked off to the Pentagon for interrogation instead.

#388 All Out

Producer: John Meredyth Lucas; Director: Paul Stanley; Writer: John Zodrow

Cast: Bob Hastings, Philip Abbott, Nan Martin, Juanita Moore, Pamela Bellwood, Eric Laneuville, Dean Santoro, Peggy Doyle, Pat Strong, Daxson Thomas, Joey Prokash

Television game show contestants are picked from an audience to see just how far their greed will take them. The game culminates with an unnerving twist on Russian Roulette.

The entertainment journal *Variety* reported that the game show depicted in this episode appeared so real to some people that, in at least one city where it aired, viewers called the broadcasting station in protest.[8]

Bob Hastings, Juanita Moore, and Eric Laneuville in All Out

#389 Out of the Depths

Producer: John Meredyth Lucas; Director: Ralph Senensky; Writer: Terry Sweeney

Cast: John Astin, Cliff DeYoung, Lynn Hamilton, John Mark Robinson, Ellen Moss, Don Miller, Nancy Adrian, Janis Lynn

A washed up, alcoholic preacher uses the word of God for booze money. Then he meets a despairing young man who has just lost his wife and child in a car accident.

Cliff DeYoung, John Astin, and Lynn Hamilton in Out of the Depths

#390 Hellbound Blues

Producer: John Meredyth Lucas; Director: Richard Bennett; Writer: J.S. Sugarhill

Cast: James McEachin, D'urville Martin, Beverly Hope Atkinson, Isabel Cooley, Stan Haze, Don Pedro Colley, Freeman King, Bob Doqui, Vince Howard, Michael Roberts, Raymond Allen, Ty Henderson

An accomplished blues singer senses the end of an era. He shocks his night club audience when he pulls out a gun and tells them he's putting on his last performance.

> Fr. Kieser's prologue to "Hellbound Blues"
>
> There are moments in the lives of all of us when nothing seems to make any sense. Work seems meaningless. Friends don't seem

to care. We feel very empty and alone. We've all known moments like this. But what happens when those moments stretch into days or weeks or months? What do we do then? Some people try to escape the feeling of desolation by denying that it's there. Others look for someone to blame for it. Still others turn in on themselves in despair and self-pity. But there is a fourth group of people who take an entirely different approach. They use the feeling of desolation to carry them beyond themselves in a silent plea for help and healing. But if we do reach beyond ourselves, is there anybody to listen? Is there anybody to come through for us?

#391 The Pendulum

Producer: John Meredyth Lucas; Director: Richard Bennett; Writer: John McGreevey

Cast: Barry Brown, John Colicos Ford Rainey, Edith Atwater, Bill Vint, Katherine Justice, Peggy Doyle, Logan Ramsey

A young mystic leaves his monastery to assume presidency of his deceased father's advertising agency. He dives into the business with trepidation and conviction, but results are mixed.

Barry Brown and John Colicos in The Pendulum

1976

As we've seen, God frequently appears as a character in *Insight* episodes. Two fine examples occur this year: in Lan O'Kun's humorous and touching "The Picture in Sobel's Window," for which he also composed the music, and John T. Dugan's comic take on *Paradise Lost*, "Jesus B.C."

Other standouts this year include: Michael Alan Humm's depiction of the therapeutic potential of psychodrama in "Rehearsal;" John McGreevey's meditation on the readiness to receive wisdom in "The Man in the Cast Iron Suit;" and Lan O'Kun's Irish tale, "For the Love of Annie."

#392 Man of The Year

Producer: John Meredyth Lucas; Director: Richard Bennett; Writer: John V. Hanrahan

Cast: Dick Gautier, Jack Carter, Steve Franken, Brooke Bundy, Allan Lurie, Jack Hanrahan, Wendell Burton, William Woodson,

The Man of the Year award is given to a top television comedian. Flashbacks, however, show he's not the man he has presented himself to be.

Fr. Kieser with cast members from Man of the Year

#393 Rehearsal

Producer: John Meredyth Lucas; Director: James Sheldon; Writer: Michael Alan Humm, Michael Jay Klassman

Cast: Cliff DeYoung, Eric Laneuville, Janet MacLachlan, Dick O'Neill, Jamie Smith Jackson, Cindy Eilbacher, Steve Benedict

Teenagers are guided through a group psychodrama session playing out their fantasies, hostilities, and misunderstandings toward their parents.

Cliff DeYoung and Jamie Smith Jackson in Rehearsal

#394 His Feet Don't Stink

Producer: John Meredyth Lucas; Director: Paul Stanley; Writer: John Zodrow

Cast: Pat Harrington, Harris Yulin, Sandy Gaviola

In a future world, an extremely wealthy man has found that his struggle for money has left him void of any true emotions. On Christmas he gets a chance to accept that fact and start over.

Pat Harrington in His Feet Don't Stink

#395 Blind Man's Bluff

Producer: John Meredyth Lucas; Director: Hal Cooper; Writer: Lan O'Kun

Cast: Rod Colbin, Ken Olfson, Ken Mars

At an annual reunion, three thieves meet to rehash their grudges and gripes against each other. One's announcement of his terminal condition changes the direction of all their lives.

Ken Olfson in Blind Man's Bluff

#396 Juvie

Producer: John Meredyth Lucas; Director: Marc Daniels; Writer: John Farrell

Cast: Michael Brandon, Michael Roberts, Ernest Thomas, Mary Alice, Tom Rosqui, William-Kirby Cullen, Chu Chu Malave

A young law student tries to humanize the penal system. He's up against violence and distrust among the youth, as well as fear and abuse among the administration.

Michael Brandon in Juvie

#397 Girl in Freefall

Producer: John Meredyth Lucas; Director: Richard Bennett; Writer: Lydia A. Wiggins

Cast: Leslie Ackerman, Jamie Smith Jackson, Mike Pataki, Bob Hogan, Lynn Carlin, Davey Davison

A sixteen-year-old girl, caught up in her family's casual and confused attitudes on sex, opts to end an unwanted pregnancy. Now she questions her choice.

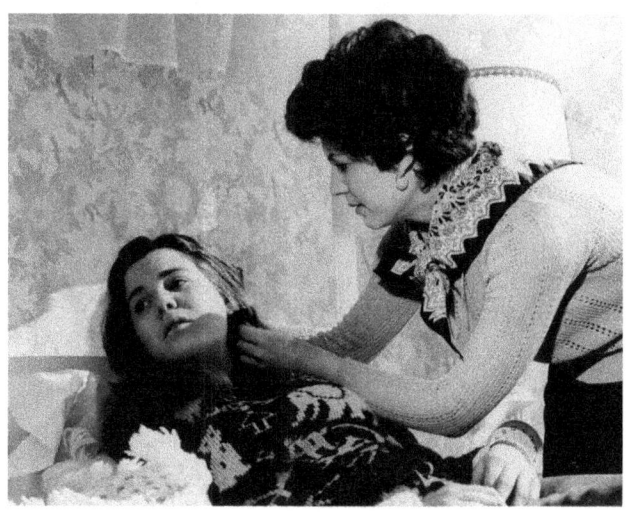

Leslie Ackerman and Lynn Carlin in Girl in Freefall

#398 The Man in the Cast Iron Suit

Producer: John Meredyth Lucas; Director: Paul Stanley; Writer: John McGreevey

Cast: John McLiam, Joshua Bryant, Michael Anderson, Jr, Susan Brown, Barry Brown, Bryan Scott, Jamie Smith Jackson

A successful businessman and his wife are faced with a conflict of values when grandpa comes to live with them. His perspective on life affects everyone, but not everyone can accept it.

John McLiam in The Man in the Cast Iron Suit

Fr, Kieser's prologue to "the Man in the Cast Iron Suit"

What makes a person wise? Is it a perspective about life, a perspective that judges everything in accordance with life's ultimate meaning and purpose? A perspective that keeps the big things big and the little things little? Is it the ability to live at peace with yourself without having to prove anything to anybody? Is it the freedom to take charge of your own life without being pulled this way and that by your own needs, desires, and compulsions? Is it your capacity to share yourself with those around you whether or not they return your love? Is wisdom something that comes with age, or is it possible for a young man or woman to become wise? Where do you get wisdom? Does it come when you root your life in that which transcends space and time, when you allow yourself to be grasped by the loving ground of your own being? Yes, what is wisdom, where do you get it, and what does it involve?

#399 Cum Laude, Come Lonely

Producer: John Meredyth Lucas; Director: John Meredyth Lucas; Writer: Lydia A. Wiggins

Cast: Gary Collins, John Megna, Beth Raines, Mariclare Costello, Ben Marley, Allan Lurie, Terry Sweeney, Danny Stern

A sensitive and intellectual teenage boy is an embarrassment to his "macho" father. Through friends, he hears the message of his own value.

#400 For the Love of Annie

Producer: John Meredyth Lucas; Director: Buzz Kulik; Writer: Lan O'Kun

Cast: John Astin, Patty Duke Astin, Harold Gould, Bob Duggan, Allan Lurie

A lonely, self-absorbed man of little means finally gets a wife, a house, and money. Now he must learn how to give and receive love.

John Astin, Patti Duke, and Fr. Kieser on the set of For the Love of Annie

#401 The Picture in Sobel's Window

Producer: John Meredyth Lucas; Director: Richard Bennett; Writer: Lan O'Kun

Cast: Beau Bridges, Ronny Cox, Robert Harris, Steve Franken, Bridget Hanley, Allan Lurie

Blinded after an eye operation, a man clings to the unreal hope that he will one day have a painting hanging in the finest art gallery in the city.

Beau Bridges and Ronny Cox in The Picture in Sobel's Window

Fr. Kieser's prologue to "The Picture in Sobel's Window"

When God created you, he had an idea of the person he wanted you to be. Your real self is to be that person in all its uniqueness. Some people discover their real selves. And so, they direct their actions and lifestyle in accordance with it. As a result, their lives take on a beautiful kind of depth and wholeness. Other people suppress their real selves. They define themselves in terms of other people's expectations. That's too bad, because our happiness is bound up with being the person God made us to be.

#402 Jesus B.C.

Producer: John Meredyth Lucas; Director: John Meredyth Lucas; Writer: John T. Dugan

Cast: William Windom, Paula Kelly, Tim Matheson, James Cromwell, Irene Tedrow

God calls a family meeting and summons his Son, "Chris," and his Holy Ghost, "Grace," to discuss how best to deal with his new creation, humanity.

Tim Matheson and Paula Kelly in Jesus, B.C.

1977

Career television writers like Charlie Hauck, Richard Fielder, and John McGreevey added to the series this year. Hauck's "A Slight Drinking Problem" spotlighted the role Al Anon can play in healing the effects of alcohol and substance abuse. Fielder's "The Alleluia Kid" examined a young athlete's ordeal with personal and family trauma. McGreevey contributed a unique Christmas episode, the dystopian "Christmas 2025."

#403 *(Lost episode)*

#404 **I Want to Die**

Producer: Mike Rhodes, Terry Sweeney; Director: Ralph Senensky; Writer: Terry Sweeney

Cast: Grant Goodeve, Jeanne Cooper, Laurie Walters, Walter Brooke

A Thanksgiving dinner turns into a nightmare as a son returns home from college and announces to his family that he's going to kill himself.

Jeanne Cooper and Grant Goodeve in I Want to Die

Fr. Kieser's prologue to "I Want to Die"

What do you and I need to live a rich and full life? First, I think we need something or someone to believe in and live for, a faith vision to give us a meaningful view of the world, and a context in which to choose our values. I also think we need a network of love relationships, a group of people who need us and whom we need. People with whom we can be ourselves and communicate honestly. People who understand and accept us as we are, and upon whom we can rely in time of trouble. I also think we need a kind of work that activates things deep within us, that enables us to express our real selves, and which not only gives us satisfaction, but enriches the lives of the people around us. But what happens to a human being who loses one or another of these things? What happens if he loses all of them? What kind of life can he have? Is it possible to rebuild it?

#405 A Slight Drinking Problem

Producer: Mike Rhodes, Terry Sweeney; Director: Hal Cooper; Writer: Charlie Hauck

Cast: Patty Duke Astin, James Hampton, Rue McClanahan, Gloria Lynn Deyer, Amzie Strickland, Charlie Hauck, Beth Raines

A wife comes to the realization that her husband has a drinking problem but can't convince him of it. To protect herself from destruction, she joins Al-Anon, an organization for relatives of alcoholics.

Patty Duke and James Hampton in A Slight Drinking Problem

> From Fr. Kieser's prologue to "A Slight Drinking Problem"
>
> In every life there are crisis points: times when we are stripped of our illusions and plunged deep within ourselves. These are moments of great danger and great opportunity. For in these moments, we must decide whether to opt for death or to embrace life in its fullness. The texture, the tone, the momentum of our whole lives are determined by these moments of decision—because we can live fully only when we have surrendered our life to life itself, only when we have allowed that higher power to take over within us...

#406 The Alleluia Kid

Producer: Mike Rhodes, Terry Sweeney; Director: Jay Sandrich; Writer: Richard Fielder

Cast: Philip Michael Thomas, Helen Martin, Diane Sommerfield, Anthony Costello, Christine Belford, Peggy Doyle

A southern black football player on the verge of a brilliant career is shattered when he is diagnosed with a muscle disorder. Through his grandmother's influence, he comes to imagine a new future for himself.

Philip Michael Thomas and Christine Belford in The Alleluia Kid

#407 She's Waiting for Us

Producer: Mike Rhodes, Terry Sweeney; Director: Richard Bennett; Writer: James McGinn

Cast: Mitch Vogel, Glynnis O'Connor, Lynn Carlin, William Schallert, Elizabeth Allen, Ron Pinkard, Laura Lacey

A teenage boy, drinking and driving, is responsible for his girlfriend's death in a car crash. At the ER, he has an out-of-body experience and sees himself, his choices, and his values in a new way.

#408 Christmas 2025

Producer: Mike Rhodes, Terry Sweeney; Director: John Meredyth Lucas; Writer: John McGreevey

Cast: James Cromwell, Elinor Donahue, Lee Purcell, Allan Lurie, Sam Groom, Sparky Marcus, Jack Hogan

It is December 25, 2025. Society has devolved to a place where human emotions and celebrations are outlawed. All personal energy must be used in State approved assignments to increase society's productivity and discipline.

Elinor Donahue and James Cromwell in Christmas 2025

#409 Leroy

Producer: Mike Rhodes, Terry Sweeney; Director: Mike Rhodes; Writer: John Zodrow

Cast: Albert Salmi, Lucille Benson, John Zoller, Woodrow Parfrey, James Doohan, Steve Franken, Shawn Shea, Roscoe Orman, Ron Sloan, Ernie Banks

An illiterate couple are not able to read a $300 medical bill. They lose their home when the State auctions it off to pay the debt.

#410 Arnstein's Miracle

Producer: Mike Rhodes, Terry Sweeney; Director: J.D. Lobue; Writer: Lan O'Kun

Cast: Howard DaSilva, David Hurst, Peter Brocco, Angela Clarke, Leon Belasco

A famous violinist believes he is becoming too ill to play. Like a miser, he hordes the few performances he thinks he has left. But, through a chance meeting with his old teacher, he remembers the joy of sharing one's gifts.

Howard DaSilva and David Hurst in Arnstein's Miracle

#411 This Side of Eden

Producer: Mike Rhodes, Terry Sweeney; Director: Jay Sandrich; Writer: Lan O'Kun

Cast: Ed Asner, Walter Matthau, Carol Burnett

Adam and Eve, guilt-stricken over Eden and appalled at Cain's murder of Abel, are alienated from each other. God decides to make an appearance to teach them something about forgiveness and reconciliation.

Walter Matthau, Carol Burnett, and Ed Asner in This Side of Eden

1978

The accomplished television writer and producer Jim Moser was one of the few creative collaborators whose work is represented over nearly the entire span of the *Insight* series, having served as a script consultant in the early 1960s, and a producer and writer into the 1980s. This year, besides producing all the episodes, he wrote "Second Chorus" about a couple who discovers that "fighting fair" is still a way of communicating. Other standouts include: John McGreevey's examination of a priest's drive for authenticity in "Is Anyone Listening?" and Leon Tokatyan's redemptive "Flawed Magi."

#412 Belfast: Black on Green

Producer: Jim Moser, Mike Rhodes; Director: Marc Daniels; Writer: William McGivern

Cast: Bob DoQui, Tim Matheson, Andy Robinson, Walter Brooke, Ford Rainey, Christine Belford, Andrew Robinson

Northern Ireland's continuing conflict climaxes in a Belfast pub as political and religious hatreds surface at gun point. A black American visitor who is caught in the middle advocates fighting for justice with "soul force."

Bob DoQui and Andy Robinson in Belfast: Black on Green

Fr. Kieser's prologue to "Belfast: Black on Green"

Northern Ireland, Lebanon, Cyprus, the Sinai, Uganda, Angola, Rhodesia, Cambodia. The world is full of trouble spots. Sometimes these conflicts have political, racial, or economic causes.

But at other times these wars are waged in the name of God. This is especially ironic, because the God worshiped by all the world's great religions is a God of love, a God who is the universal father of all mankind. He is a God who wants his children to live at peace with one another. He outlaws violence. He forbids hatred. This is why to justify the killing of another human being in the name of God is to take God's name in vain. There is no such thing as a holy war. But what do you do in the face of injustice? When your rights are denied and your dignity is assaulted? You can't just sit back and allow yourself to be exploited. Is there any way to struggle against injustice without violence and without hatred?

#413 The Rebirth of Packy Rowe

Producer: Jim Moser, Mike Rhodes; Director: Jay Sandrich; Writer: Lan O'Kun

Cast: Jack Klugman, Bob Newhart, Larry Gelman, Steve Franken

Theatrical agent Packy Rowe has a low opinion of himself and what he's done with his life. He's in for a few surprises when he dies and meets God who thinks otherwise.

Jack Klugman and Bob Newhart in The Rebirth of Packy Rowe

#414 Is Anyone Listening?

Producer: Jim Moser, Mike Rhodes; Director: John Meredyth Lucas; Writer: John McGreevey

Cast: Martin Sheen, Greg Mullavey, Eugene Roche, Eve Plumb, Peggy Doyle

A middle-aged priest brings his personal struggles to therapy. He painfully explores his role as the "prefect priest," and his need to be fully himself.

Eve Plumb and Martin Sheen in Is Anyone Listening?

#415 Just Before Eve

Producer: Jim Moser, Mike Rhodes; Director: Jay Sandrich; Writer: Lan O'Kun

Cast: Matin Sheen, Flip Wilson, Darleen Carr, Henry Proach

Adam is bored, roaming the Garden of Eden alone and unsettled. God challenges him to seek out the cause of his distress. They finally come up with a solution.

Flip Wilson in Just Before Eve

Fr. Kieser's prologue to "Just Before Eve"

Sometimes you and I get bored. Why? Why do we get bored? I think we get bored because we neglect our own growth, because we are not using the full capacity, the powers God has given us to grow and develop, and become the open, aware, free, creative, loving human beings he made us to be. So, what are these powers we're to use? Intelligence, by which we explore the world around us, and the even more fascinating world inside us. Free will, by which we take charge of our own lives, select their goals, determine their values, and decide how, when and with whom we will express ourselves. And heart, by which we reach out in love to share ourselves with our brother and sister human beings. You and I are surrounded by human beings who need us. People with whom we can share ourselves.

#416 Flawed Magi

Producer: Jim Moser, Mike Rhodes; Director: Joel Zwick; Writer: Leon Tokatyan

Cast: Bo Svenson, Julius Harris, Clifford David, Normann Burton, Albert Reed, Gordon Hurst, Sandy Kenyon

A famous country western singer makes his annual "charity" visit to the county jail. But when he is able to admit that he is doing the right thing for the wrong reasons, he truly has something to give.

#417 Second Chorus

Producer: Jim Moser, Mike Rhodes; Director: Russ Petranto; Writer: Jim Moser

Cast: John Astin, Patty Duke Astin, Wesley Eure, Marcia Wallace, Raymond Duke

A couple who has undergone a "successful divorce" come together to attend their son's wedding. When the wedding doesn't happen, they talk about their own rocky relationship and decide to pave the way for reconciliation.

Marcia Wallace in Second Chorus

"Fr. Kieser…he was a buddy of mine. And every once in a while, he'd drop by and put another script on the kitchen table. And how do you say no to Fr. Kieser?"⁹

Patty Duke

1979

Beginning this year, Fr. Kieser's appearances on screen to provide commentary on episodes became more rare. Another opening animation appeared, without any introductory remarks.

Familiar *Insight* themes are exemplified in William McGivern's "Plus Time Served," about an individual's change of heart and stance against institutional injustice; Richard Fielder's "The Man Who Mugged God," a parable of the effects of God's love; and James McGinn's and Ellwood Kieser's "A Slight Change in Plans," which takes spiritual experiences and values seriously.

#418 Plus Time Served

Producer: Mike Rhodes, Jim Moser; Director: Ralph Senensky; Writer: William McGivern

Cast: James Farentino, Don Stroud, Gregory Sierra, Christine Belford, Walter Brooke, Julius Harris

When a popular newscaster is summoned to mediate a prison riot, he is forced to grow beyond his self-centered existence. A betrayal of trust puts his new-found awareness to the test.

Gregory Sierra and Julius Harris in Plus Time Served

"The elimination by the networks of the anthology format from their schedules was artistically unfortunate. True, there were still some series that managed to produce provocative dramas, but those were restricted by their continuing series format. I think that is an additional reason why *Insight* was such an important part of American television programming... Regarding our country's immigration problem, medical problems, and our situation with the poor, *Insight* was not only current—it was uncannily prescient."

Ralph Senensky, Director

#419 The Man Who Mugged God

Producer: Mike Rhodes, Jim Moser; Director: Marc Daniels; Writer: Richard Fielder

Cast: Harold Gould, Warren Oates

A desperate and despairing junkie mugs a blind beggar at knife point. The beggar slowly reveals how much he knows him, loves him, and cares about how he will live the rest of his life.

Harold Gould and Warren Oats in The Man Who Mugged God

#420 A Slight Change in Plans

Producer: Mike Rhodes; Director: Mike Rhodes; Writer: James McGinn, Ellwood Kieser

Cast: Howard McGillin, Andrew Duggan, Bethel Leslie, Jerry Houser, Noelle North, Anthony Costello

A young salesman has a promising career prepared for him in the family's business. After a trip to Latin America and working in a barrio, he reconsiders his life direction and contemplates a vocation to the priesthood.

Andrew Duggan in A Slight Change of Plans

#421 Checkmate

Producer: Mike Rhodes; Director: Jay Sandrich; Writer: Lan O'Kun

Cast: Bruce Davison, Efrem Zimbalist, Jr., Rebecca Balding, Janice Kent, William Zuchart

An egotistical man wants the perfect relationship, so God gives him a woman robot. Ultimately, he discovers that what he really wants involves vulnerability and imperfection.

Efrem Zimbalist, Jr., Bruce Davison, and Rebecca Balding in Checkmate

#422 Holy Moses

Producer: Mike Rhodes; Director: Hal Cooper; Writer: Lan O'Kun

Cast: Vincent Gardenia, Harold Gould, Warren Berlinger

Moses and his brother Aaron wish they could find purpose and a land "flowing with milk and honey." Then, God, in a top hat and suit, asks a reluctant Moses to liberate his people from Egypt.

Vincent Gardenia and Harold Gould in Holy Moses

1980

Two of Fr. Kieser's own scripts were produced this year as "*Insight* Specials": "Resurrection," a powerful Holy Week reflection on the temptations of Christ, long before Martin Scorsese took up the theme; and "God in the Dock," a courtroom drama treating what theologians refer to as theodicy, or "the problem of evil."

Other highlights from this year: William McGivern's "Cargoes," a tale of the complexities involved in humanitarian outreach in post-colonial Africa; Christopher Keane's "Mr. and Mrs. Bliss," dealing with pain and resilience in adult life; and John McGreevey's "Thea," a spiritual meditation on masculine and feminine energies.

#423 Cargoes

Producer: Mike Rhodes; Director: Marc Daniels; Writer: William McGivern

Cast: Emily Yancy, Raymond St. Jacques, Scott Hylands, Stephan Keep, Parley Baer, James A. Watson, Jr., Rock Birt, Lawrence Mandley

A chartered plane carrying two famine relief workers, a mercenary, and a businessman is shot down over West Africa by the leader of a guerilla band. A brutal contest of wills ensues.

Stephan Keep and Emily Yancy in Cargoes

#424 Mr. And Mrs. Bliss

Producer: Mike Rhodes; Director: Paul Stanley; Writer: Christopher Keane

Cast: Donna Mills, Lawrence Pressman, Nita Talbot, A Martinez

A husband is refused tenure at the university. He wants to run away from the pain and disappointment but is reminded that new life can emerge from loss, and that strength and support come from marriage.

A Martinez and Nita Talbot in Mr. and Mrs. Bliss

#425 *(Lost episode)*

#426 **Long Road Home**

Producer: Mike Rhodes; Director: Hal Cooper; Writer: Lan O'Kun

Cast: Martin Sheen, Harold Gould, Emilio Estevez

Filled with self-doubt, a man panics and walks out on his fiancé the night before their wedding. A conversation with God in a deserted motel gives him a new sense of possibility and fidelity in life.

Martin Sheen and Harold Gould in Long Road Home

"It was like doing a little play in a week's time. You got to rehearse and form a full character... You formed a community with players, and many of them you'd see again and again. There were some wonderful actors, and they were always so pleased to do it. It was great fun, because you got a chance to play characters you wouldn't ordinarily get to do...

"It was a moral theme, but it was nondenominational. It didn't beat people over the head with how they should act or how they ought to feel. It just presented a very human situation in a realistic setting. And sometimes a very poetic setting, a very humorous setting. It was always about being human, about being vulnerable.

It was about being of service, being generous... That was always a welcome relief over all the other stuff you had to do on television."

Martin Sheen

#427 Resurrection

Producer: Ellwood Kieser; Director: John Meredyth Lucas; Writer: Ellwood Kieser

Cast: Richard Beymer, James Farentino, Joanna Cassidy

The time is Good Friday afternoon. The place is limbo. The person is Jesus of Nazareth, shortly after his crucifixion. With him are two demons intent on blocking his resurrection.

Richard Beymer and Joanna Cassidy in Resurrection

From Fr. Keiser's script for "Resurrection"

Jesus: Well, you see my Father has a lot of children. They're very beautiful, I mean, people are terrific. I couldn't get enough of them, especially the kids and the poor...

Psychologist: You were telling me about the job your Father had given you.

Jesus: Yeah, well, you see these people are very beautiful, but they are also screwed up. Way back, a bunch of them goofed, threw sand in the gears. The result is a quirk in the evolutionary process.

Psychologist: A quirk in the evolutionary process?

Jesus: That's right. They're very beautiful but they don't know they're beautiful. So, they end up doing ugly things.

Psychologist: Like?

Jesus: Like putting each other down, degrading themselves. Like pushing my Father away.

Psychologist: And what is the cause of this sad state of affairs?

Jesus: Don't you see? They have trouble loving each other because they don't love themselves. They don't love themselves because they have forgotten how much my Father loves them.

Psychologist: So?

Jesus: So, my job was to remind them of my Father's love and help them feel it.

Psychologist: And did you do that?

Jesus: I tried to do it. Maybe if I can just get back, I can finish the job.

#428 God in the Dock

Producer: Mike Rhodes; Director: Paul Stanley; Writer: Ellwood Kieser

Cast: Della Reese, Don Stroud, Ellen Geer, Howard McGillin, Peter Haskell, Richard Beymer, Marcia Rodd, Ray Duke, Patricia Mitchell

In a class action suit, God is placed on trial for all the pain, injustice and misery suffered by humanity. Then the plaintiffs start to take matters into their own hands.

Della Reese in God in the Dock

#429 Thea

Producer: Mike Rhodes; Director: Mike Rhodes; Writer: John McGreevey

Cast: Julie Sommars, Jess Walton, Alan Feinstein, Patricia Eltinge

A mysterious woman named Thea enters the lives of a young married couple. The man, a mathematician, is compelled to accept the feminine side of himself, while the woman comes to embrace her inner power.

Julie Sommers and Jess Walton in Thea

#430 Goodbye

Producer: Mike Rhodes; Director: Richard Bennett; Writer: Lan O'Kun

Cast: Richard Benjamin, Ramon Bieri, James Callahan, Davey Davison, Barney Phillips, Jim Neely, Tom Fitzpatrick

A writer's twelve-year-old son is dying of cancer, and he is unwilling to let go of him. In a dream, his own father comes to his aid.

#431 Unfinished Business

Producer: Judy Greening; Director: Ralph Senensky; Writer: James McGinn

Cast: Jack Bannon, Bill Quinn, Marcia Rodd, Steven Vegh

A very successful Los Angeles businessman has neglected his elderly father who lives in a retirement home in Chicago. After the older man's heart attack, they rediscover each other, and a new and deeper relationship forms between father and son.

Jack Bannon on the set of Unfinished Business

"I wrote a bunch of scripts for Paulist over the years... 'Unfinished Business' was the true story of my father... One year he had a heart attack...damn near died in the hospital. He stayed with us for a period of months, and I became his male nurse. He showed a vulnerability he never did before. He was always a proud man. And I decided to interview him. Since he knew this was it, he wasn't afraid to really open up...

"Paulist was wonderful. It was always unique... Most of them were good and most of the competition was sermons. Throw in *Insight* where you had name actors doing real drama. It's been a very important part of my life."

James McGinn, writer

1981

Mike Rhodes had a major part to play in the later years of *Insight*, serving as producer and sometimes director of episodes. He would go on to guide numerous projects for Paulist Productions after *Insight* as well.

Comedy and drama were well represented in this year's slate. One of Lan O'Kun's finest episodes, "The Sixth Day," is a comic take on human consciousness; while Ellwood Kieser's "Missing Person's Bureau" takes a humorous premise to heart-rending lengths. Carol Evan McKeand's "The Needle's Eye," and John McGreevey's "God's Guerillas" are examples of personal struggles within social hardship.

Fr. Kieser's commentary returned as a regular feature of the program.

#432 When Heroes Fall

Producer: Mike Rhodes; Director: Mike Rhodes; Writer: James Moser

Cast: Jose Perez, Panchito Gomez, Karmin Murcelo, Arlene Golonka, Emilio Estevez, Edgardo Ramon

For seventeen-year-old David, his dad is the greatest. When he discovers that his father is involved with another woman, his emotional universe is shattered.

Panchito Gomez and Jose Perez in When Heroes Fall

#433 *(Lost episode)*

#434 The Sixth Day

Producer: Mike Rhodes, Terry Sweeney; Director: Richard Bennett; Writer: Lan O'Kun

Cast: Randolph Mantooth, Marty Feldman, Keenan Wynn, James Callahan

On the sixth day God created man. With the help of a wacky angel, God puts the finishing touches on his finest creation.

Randolph Mantooth, Keenan Wynn, and Marty Feldman in The Sixth Day

#435 The Needle's Eye

Producer: Mike Rhodes, Terry Sweeney; Director: Robert Butler; Writer: Carol Evan McKeand

Cast: Ron Howard, Jerry Houser, Nan Martin, Rahsaan Morris, Candace Bowen

Two medical students on an excursion to Africa are forced to seek help when their jeep breaks down in a poor village. Faced with the disease and poverty, the two friends struggle with their dream of the good life and the reality of the suffering they see.

#436 Missing Persons Bureau

Producer: Mike Rhodes, Terry Sweeney; Director: Linda Day; Writer: Ellwood Kieser

Cast: Alan Feinstein, Hector Elizondo, Christine Belford, Greg Zadikov, Lew Brown, Kit McDonough, Niall Gartlan

A man returns from a tour of duty in Vietnam to face his son's death and wife's infidelity. He goes to a missing persons bureau for help in finding God.

Alan Feinstein and Hector Elizondo in Missing Persons Bureau

#437 The Domino Effect

Producer: Mike Rhodes, Terry Sweeney; Director: Joe Gannon; Writer: William McGivern

Cast: Jan Clayton, Greg Mullavey, Gene Roche, Stephen Keep, Bob Doqui, Joe Spano, Pam McMyler, Lynn Hamilton

Residents of a poor neighborhood protest when the president of a supermarket chain decides to close their branch. When the president's mother, one of the company's principal stockholders, joins the protest, he retaliates by challenging her mental competency in court.

Gene Roche in The Domino Effect

Fr Kieser's prologue to "The Domino Effect"

All of us in one way or another, work. And our jobs are a very important part of our lives. While it's true that we are good apart from what we do, it's also true that our inherent dignity not only expresses itself in our work, but it can and should be enhanced by that work. Your job not only enables you to support your family, it also can and should enable you to grow and develop and become more fully human. This is why you should look for a job that will stimulate your mind and challenge your will. A job that enables you to exercise your initiative and assume responsibility. A job that you believe in, that helps you contribute to the lives of other people. Such a job may be demanding, but it will not be boring. Work isn't supposed to be drudgery. Even if hard, it should occasion satisfaction and even joy...

#438 God's Guerillas

Producer: Mike Rhodes, Terry Sweeney; Director: Delbert Mann; Writer: John McGreevey

Cast: Patty Duke Astin, James Farentino, Sherry Hursey, Bibi Besch, A Martinez, Michael Pataki, Domingo Ambriz

When a convent in El Salvador is occupied by a fleeing band of Marxist guerillas, both sisters and soldiers find their ideals challenged.

James Farentino in God's Guerillas

#439 Rendezvous

Producer: Mike Rhodes, Terry Sweeney; Director: J.D. Lobue; Writer: David C. Field

Cast: James Farentino, Melinda Dillon

A successful businessman, suffering an anxiety attack, escapes to a remote resort where he encounters a mysterious woman. Not knowing who she is or where she came from, he is baffled by her apparent knowledge of his past.

James Farentino and Melinda Dillon in Rendezvous

Fr Kieser's prologue to "Rendezvous"

For centuries we were taught that to be a woman was to be tender, intuitive, and spontaneous; and that to be a man was to be aggressive, rational, and controlled. But now we know that in everyone man there is a woman, and in every woman there is a man. Does this surprise you? It shouldn't. For the integrally human is neither masculine alone nor feminine alone. It is masculine and feminine in relationship. The man who is whole will be in touch with his compassionate and emotional side. And the woman who is whole will be in touch with her assertive, take-charge side. Neither will be embarrassed to express the opposite side of themselves. For he knows that his masculinity is increased rather than diminished by the presence of the feminine within him; and she knows that her femininity is heightened rather than compromised by the presence of the masculine within her. The masculine and feminine in relationship—this is the characteristic of an emotionally healthy human being.

#440 Little Miseries

Producer: Mike Rhodes, Terry Sweeney, Marina Angelini; Director: Jay Sandrich; Writer: Ben Elisco

Cast: John Ritter, Audra Lindley, Edward Andrews, Stephanie Faracy

A young man raised by his manipulative aunt comes to realize that her scheming is keeping both of them from the love that they need.

Audra Lindley and John Ritter in Little Miseries

#441 A Decision to Love

Producer: Mike Rhodes, Terry Sweeney; Director: Buzz Kulik; Writer: Richard Fielder

Cast: Melinda Dillon, David Spielberg, Ellen Geer, Gregory Sierra, Joshua Bryant, Ed Grover, Edith Diaz

Tom and Janet share a house, a bed, a bank account, and kids, but they never share themselves. Then they attend a "Marriage Encounter" weekend where they take off their masks and experience the joy of emotional intimacy.

David Spielberg and Melinda Dillon in A Decision to Love

#442 Teddy

Producer: Mike Rhodes, Terry Sweeney; Director: Mike Rhodes; Writer: Lan O'Kun

Cast: Bud Cort, June Lockhart, Sam Gilman, Carol Androsky

A 29-year-old man who was born with a misshapen face suffers alone. His mother is so ashamed of him that she keeps him locked in the house to protect him from cruelty and ridicule. Then he decides to risk being seen.

Sam Gilman and Bud Cort in Teddy

1982

Special mention should be made of Jane Murray, casting director for *Insight* from 1965 till its conclusion. Her contribution is seen in the array of actors who starred on the show throughout the years. Like so many other collaborators on the series, she had an accomplished television career and worked on a number of successful shows.

One cannot watch James McGinn's "Every Ninety Seconds" without thinking of the pressures Paulist Productions was experiencing at this time due to the loss of support for public-interest television programming.

Other highlights this year include: Korby Siamis' "Matchpoint," a smart and humorous take on relationships in a high-tech setting; and John Sacret Young's "Leave Me Alone, God," a deep dive into a dour rationalist's struggle for his humanity. Josef Anderson's "White Star Garage" may be the series' most memorable Christmas episode. It was also the twelfth and last episode overseen by the acclaimed television director Ralph Senensky.

#443 The Fiddler

Producer: Mike Rhodes, Terry Sweeney; Director: Marc Daniels; Writer: Ellwood Kieser

Cast: Melinda Dillon, Stephan Keep, Greg Mullavey, Shony Braun, Christine Belford, Julie Cobb, Rick Lenz

Three celebrating couples are serenaded by a gypsy fiddler. Some of them hear his music. Others do not. As the evening crescendos, we being to understand why.

Melinda Dillon and Shony Braun in The Fiddler

#444 White Star Garage

Producer: Mike Rhodes, Terry Sweeney; Director: Ralph Senensky; Writer: Josef Anderson

Cast: Fausto Bara, Christine Avila, Elisha Cook, Peter White, Maria Grimm, Patti Dixon

On Christmas Eve, Jose Lopez and his expectant wife Maria navigate a city of cold hearts. When Maria begins a difficult labor, Jose must face his distrust of the world and seek help.

> "One of the things that Bud said to me was that we had a kind of freedom that other commercial venues do not have: 'We don't have sponsors. We are our own sponsor. And as a result, we can talk about the theme and talk about it freely'... That we never would find in commercial television or film... I'm very grateful to *Insight* for such great stories."
>
> Christine Avila

#445 Matchpoint

Producer: Mike Rhodes, Terry Sweeney; Director: Will MacKenzie; Writer: Korby Siamis

Cast: Kay Lenz, Robert Pine, Nancy Holbrook

A man has had fourteen computer dates in fourteen days with no luck. But he refuses to take advice from Compu-Date's president, who has relationship issues of her own.

Kay Lenz in Matchpoint

#446 Every Ninety Seconds

Producer: Mike Rhodes, Terry Sweeney; Director: Mike Rhodes; Writer: James McGinn

Cast: William Wintersole, Greg Mullavey, Sam Chew, Christine Avila, Carol Mallory, Conrad Janis

Channel Three is finally number one in the ratings. But when its popular news coverage grows increasingly exploitive, the station's manager faces the toughest decision of his career.

> **Fr. Kieser's prologue to "Every Ninety Seconds"**
>
> We turn on television to be entertained. But the fact of the matter is: while we're being entertained, we are also being either enriched or degraded. How can television enrich us? By telling us stories that make us proud to be human beings, that give us an experience of the humanity of people very different from ourselves, that challenge us to go deep and use our freedom in an enlightened, responsible, and loving way. How can television degrade us? By making us want things we don't need. By telling us we are failures as human beings if we don't have what it is selling. By helping us escape into a world of illusion. By catering to our baser instincts. Television can either enrich or degrade. This means that the people who decide what will be aired have great power. But they also have a very great responsibility. And so do we as viewers. What should we watch, and what should we refuse to watch?

#447 A Gun for Mandy

Producer: Mike Rhodes, Terry Sweeney; Director: Ted Post; Writer: David C. Field

Cast: Lois Nettleton, Anthony Costello, Lance Kerwin, Ellen Geer, Jim Antonio

Mandy is terrified. The man who frightened her at the bookstore has appeared at her home. Reluctantly, she accepts her neighbor's offer of a gun.

Lance Kerwin in A Gun for Mandy

#448 So Little Time

Producer: Mike Rhodes, Terry Sweeney; Director: Richard Bennett; Writer: Lan O'Kun

Cast: William Devane, Lois Nettleton, David Speilberg, Sally Kirkland, Sam Chew, Allan Lurie

Caught in the crossfire of a civil war, a famous correspondent has only an hour to live. With minutes left, he can finally relate to a wife he never really appreciated.

Lois Nettleton and William Devane in So Little Time

#449 For Love or Money

Producer: Mike Rhodes, Terry Sweeney; Director: J.D. Lobue; Writer: Lan O'Kun

Cast: Allan Rich, Steve Landesberg, Michael Lembeck, Maggie Roswell

A millionaire miser, Philodeon K. Acrimonious, is amused by his new doctor, Gideon O. Dominicus, until Gideon gives Phil his diagnosis. Now Phil needs something he can't buy.

#450 Leave Me Alone, God

Producer: Mike Rhodes, Terry Sweeney; Director: Mike Rhodes; Writer: John Sacret Young

Cast: Richard Jordan, Louise Sorel, Grant Goodeve, Laurie Prange, Kyle Spicer

Philosophy professor Jeb Buckley is part showman, part iconoclast. He plays games with his wife and students, promising much, delivering little. Then, with a female student, he gets in over his head.

Richard Jordan in Leave Me Alone, God

"*Insight* was interesting because Bud wanted it to not be 'Catholic' with a large 'C' but 'catholic' with a small 'c'... You felt like you were reaching after better or deeper stuff inside yourself."

John Sacret Young

1983

The last year of *Insight*, with only six episodes, sustained its acumen for exploring personal, communal, social, and spiritual issues with humor, intelligence, and drama. Josef Anderson's "Dutton's Choice" makes its case for compassion in the workplace in the face of the need for efficiency; David Field's "Hit Man" is a serious study of a difficult and easily avoided social issue; and Pamela Douglas' "Butterfly" tells a tender story of grief and renewal.

Although *Insight* ended this year, Paulist Productions continued to produce syndicated television programming in its mold, especially geared to teen audiences. Fr. Kieser remained President of the company and producer of television and film projects till his death in 2000.

#451 Dutton's Choice.

Producer: Mike Rhodes, Terry Sweeney; Director: Ted Post; Writer: Josef Anderson

Cast: Nicholas Pryor, Barbara Sharma, Dana Elcar, Nedra Volz, Nita Talbot

A fantasy about a hospital administrator who values production over people. His obsession for efficiency destroys morale, until he gets down into the trenches with everyone else.

Nicholas Pryor in Dutton's Choice

#452 The Day Everything Went Wrong

Producer: Mike Rhodes, Terry Sweeney; Director: Jay Sandrich; Writer: Ellwood Kieser

Cast: Dick Van Patten, Beverly Garland, Joel Higgins, Florence Halop, Robbie Rist

Thanksgiving approaches but Joey doesn't feel he has anything to be thankful for. In fact, this is the worst day of his life. A visit from God gives him a new outlook on life.

Joel Higgins and Dick Van Patten in The Day Everything Went Wrong

From Fr. Kieser's script for "The Day Everything Went Wrong"

God: Joey, for a long time now you haven't liked yourself. And not liking yourself you haven't liked me. Because, you see, I not only made you, I am the center of your real self. You spent your whole life running away, Joey, trying to be someone you're not. There's nothing wrong with selling cars, but there is something wrong with what it meant to you.

Joey: What do you mean?

God: It was your means of escape. Every time you sold one you said to yourself, See, I'm not as bad as I think I am. I'm good for something after all. And you kept saying that instead of taking a real look at yourself. If you had, you'd see what I made. You'd see what I see.

Joey: Which is?

God: A photostat of me. A very beautiful human being.

#453 The Clearing House

Producer: Mike Rhodes, Terry Sweeney; Director: Will MacKenzie; Writer: Ben Elisco

Cast: Richard Kline, Ed Begley, Jr., Judith-Marie Bergan, Ernest Harden, Jr., Olivia Barash

When a prostitute offers a Christmas gift to a teenage halfway house, she sets off a chain of very different reactions: from judgment, to compassion, to transformation.

#454 Hit Man

Producer: Mike Rhodes, Terry Sweeney; Director: Norman Lloyd; Writer: David Field

Cast: Efrem Zimbalist, Jr., Patty Duke Astin, John Anderson, Al Ruscio

Four people stranded in an airport. One man is a hired killer. An unusual twist has the group wondering about their complicity in the act.

Patty Duke, Al Ruscio, and Efrem Zimbalist, Jr. in Hit Man

#455 The Game Room

Producer: Mike Rhodes, Terry Sweeney; Director: Mike Rhodes; Writer: Leon Tokatyan, Diana Bell Tokatyan

Cast: Melinda Dillon, Max Gail, Richard Schaal, Richard Dysart, Leon Askin, Richard Libertini,

In the backroom of a video store, Russian and U.S. leaders play a high stakes game with nuclear warheads. Minutes from the destruction of the world, a woman wanders in to ask unnerving questions on behalf of humanity.

Richard Dysart and Richard Schaal in The Game Room

#456 Butterfly

Producer: Mike Rhodes, Terry Sweeney; Director: Mike Rhodes; Writer: Pamela Douglas

Cast: Rosanna Arquette, Christine Avila, David Thomas, Wendy Smith Howard

A passionate young woman is devastated after the death of her newborn child. Through honesty, vulnerability, and openness to those who want to help, she is able to find spiritual rebirth.

178 • INSIGHT

Fr. Kieser, C.S.P.

- III -
After *Insight*

Production on *Insight* ended in 1983. Although the Board of Paulist Productions was willing to fight on, Fr. Kieser understood that the days when broadcasters would provide free public service airtime to non-profit groups were coming to an end. He was not as despondent about ending the show as one might think. The question that filled his mind at the time was: "What next?"

His answer was to sail into mainstream American broadcasting, attempting to find a place for his brand of religious/values-based programming in the highly competitive secular media world. This would mean finding high-concept stories with bankable stars, but could that be done? Based on the network of contacts in the industry that Fr. Bud had built over the years, it was worth a try.

Even before *Insight* had ended, Fr. Kieser developed a deal with the Capital Cities media group to produce half-hour syndicated television specials for teenagers known as the "Family Specials." They aired in the early evenings and even helped some notable actors launch their careers: Emilio Estevez, Judge Reinhold, Lara Dern, and Charlie Sheen among them. A teen-oriented television series, *Buchanan High*, was also attempted, but delivered only four episodes. Fr. Bud then produced three hour-long specials for Capital Cities: *The Girl on the Edge of Town* about teen pregnancy, *High Powder* on drug abuse, and *The Juggler of Notre Dame*, a story based on a medieval legend. That film became a Christmas special that was rebroadcast for several years. A prime-time Easter special followed, *The Fourth Wiseman*, based on a story by Henry van Dyke, and starring Martin Sheen and Alan Arkin. All these productions span the years from 1977 to 1985.

When support for hour-long specials seemed to wane, Fr. Bud moved on to two-hour television movie ideas. He began the arduous process of pitching story ideas to development directors and producers at the TV networks. Finally, in 1985, he got some interest in a script about an American doctor who confronts the human suffering brought on by the Ethiopian famine that had shocked the world at that time. After a tumultuous production process, *We Are the Children*, starring Ally Sheedy and Ted Danson, aired on ABC in 1987.

Fr. Bud wanted to tell the stories of heroes, but his ideas seemed too controversial to the television executives he talked to. To make the films he wanted to, he would have to raise the funding and bring all the creative elements together himself. Two feature films followed. The first was 1989's *Romero*, starring Raul Julia, about the trials and transformation of the Archbishop of El Salvador during that country's brutal civil war. The success of that effort, in terms of its production process and critical reception, paved the way for *Entertaining Angels: The Dorothy Day Story*. That film, released in 1996, starred Moira Kelly in the role of the renowned Catholic social activist in depression-era New York.

Fr. Bud kept planning and collaborating on projects till his death on September 16, 2000. Paulist Productions has continued to produce films, documentaries, and digital media in the spirit of its founder's Christian and humanistic principles. The entertainment landscape may keep changing, but the work of inviting people to explore their lives in a way that leads to deeper awareness, purpose, inspiration, and hope goes on.

-IV-

Epilogue: The Spirituality of the "Hollywood Priest"

I worked for a brief time with Fr. Ellwood Kieser as the Director of Creative Development at Paulist Productions. In a discussion we once had about his work in the entertainment field, he said to me: "The more secular the world becomes, the more hungry it is for symbols of transcendence." I can quote him here because I wrote down those words right after he said them. I've since used them (with attribution) in classes I've taught to screenwriters and aspiring filmmakers, as well as to theology students.

The question of spirituality is one that touches on how human beings and communities discover and relate to the transcendent, the divine. How do we relate to the mystery that surrounds our existence, a mystery that is both beyond us and within us? What experiences awaken and nurture that relationship?

No one can adequately summarize that reality for another person. It is too profound and dynamic to capture in a few words. But I would like to attempt to point out some of the streams that may have fed into that great life-giving river in Fr. Bud's life.

"Gospel Density"

The first thing that can be said about Fr. Bud's spirituality is that, as a priest, it was centered on proclaiming the Word of God, celebrating the sacraments, and spiritually accompanying people. As a

Paulist, a member of the Missionary Society of St. Paul the Apostle, the first American order of priests, he was especially interested in communicating the gospel message in ways that the contemporary world could appreciate. When he discovered the power of drama to engage people on the deepest levels, but also the costs involved in media endeavors, he came up with criteria for deciding what he would produce. Chief among them was what he called "gospel density." To justify the resources needed to produce his films, Fr. Bud wanted to tell stories that had a potential for illuminating gospel values and giving viewers an experience of God's presence in the human situation.

This clearly didn't mean only producing shows with explicit religious or biblical content. He did make those kinds of films, like the television movie *The Fourth Wiseman*, or his documentary *The Jesus Experience* about the figure of Jesus in art history. Yet, "gospel density" extended further, to the questions raised by a story and the conversations that could follow it. Fr. Bud was passionate about how God's wisdom could be uncovered in the human condition. The "good news" had to be seen, touched, and felt in real lives. Christ, who said, *"I came so that they might have life and have it more abundantly"* (Jn 10:10), revealed himself in human pains, joys, and struggles, and that's where Fr. Bud wanted to look.

Entertaining and Enriching

Fr. Kieser had a rich intellectual life that he nourished with reading and study. He received a doctorate from the Graduate Theological Union in Berkeley, and later taught at Claremont and UCLA. The title of his dissertation was "Cinema as Religious Experience." In it he presented his ideas about the interpersonal nature of cinema and its ability to elicit ultimate concerns. He argued that life involves a long and tough process of "humanization" in which we search for meaning and become freer and more loving. We aren't alone in this process. God is intimately involved every step of the way.

Fr. Bud believed that art, including good television, can assist this process of humanization by distilling reality in a way that reveals meaning and helps viewers grapple with their deepest questions and needs. It can help us understand ourselves better, appreciate our common humanity with those who are different, and motivate us to reach out to others in love. This became Fr. Bud's passion: to delve into both comedy and drama as instruments to assist God's work in human souls.

Faithful and Free

In episodes of *Insight* that feature priests prominently (e.g., "A Slight Change in Plans," "The 34th Hour," "Is Anyone Listening?"), one can sense Fr. Bud's own vocational story—his soaring commitment, as well as his personal struggles. In his on-camera commentary, as well as in the striking questions posed by his dramas, one can appreciate his deep commitment to scripture and the tradition of the church. He fiercely defended faith against dogmatic secularism and its authoritarian cousins. He made the case for traditional morality and social ethics, but never by creating straw figures that could easily be knocked down. He confronted the best opposing arguments with his own sharp intellect and pastoral sense.

Yet, the themes Fr. Bud gravitated to also show his willingness to re-examine traditional expectations and roles. In the parlance of the second Vatican Council, he sought to read "the signs of the times," prompting him to challenge social structures that he saw as offending human dignity. He was critical of church figures whose rigidity forced them to look fearfully backward rather than courageously forward. His Paulist spirituality, rooted in devotion to the Holy Spirit, drew out of him a trust in the Spirit's guidance. It gave him freedom to delve inward through experiences of therapy and prayer. It also gave him courage to reach outward and to embrace needed change during a tumultuous social period.

Building Community

Fr. Kieser's vision was not limited to what he alone could accomplish. He wanted to partner with others in the entertainment industry to create good products that would have a positive influence in the world. To watch Fr. Bud on a working film set was to see a man fully alive and engaged. For him, though, the values in a television show or movie began with the writer, so he wanted to especially highlight and support that role. In 1974, he founded the "Humanitas Prize" for "humanizing achievement in writing." He hoped to encourage screenwriting that communicated values, formed consciences, and motivated people to become more compassionate and forgiving. The Prize continues to this day, offering awards in television and film categories.

Fr. Bud also wanted to provide young writers with mentorship from established screenwriters. He initiated the "Humanitas Master Writers' Workshops" as a way for them to share ideas. In this venue he shared his own thoughts about how writers need to activate all the layers of their own humanity in order to reach the depths within their audience. For him, the path to a fuller life meant being open to authentic experiences of friendship, community, family life, meaningful work, play, humility, wonder, suffering, and solitude. He urged writers to walk a path of prayer. He himself remained faithful to the practice of praying in solitude for an hour every day.

The Poor and Marginalized

Fr. Bud interacted with many of the elite in Hollywood and the wider Los Angeles cultural scene. But he was never taken in by the trappings of wealth and privilege. When he felt the need for perspective, he would go to L.A.'s Skid Row to serve meals to the homeless. He chose to minister not only in well-to-do parishes, but also to needy communities in the inner city. He chose dramatic themes that challenged social complacency and confronted issues of poverty, racism, and war. He was acutely aware of the need to raise money from donors for his work, but always tested himself by saying: "This is money that belongs to the poor."

He was not an armchair activist. When devastating famines hit Africa in the early 1980s, he took actors like John Amos, Patty Duke, and Cliff Robertson with him to Somalia, Kenya, and Ethiopia to see and hear for themselves the stories of suffering people. The television movie *We Are the Children* was a result. He also contracted malaria. Then, in 1983, when he made the bold move to produce his first feature film, *Romero*, about the martyred Archbishop of El Salvador, he took his screenwriter, John Sacret Young, with him to the civil war-torn country to interview both friends and foes of the archbishop. They saw firsthand the results of the death squads that persecuted the common people. He came back with a stronger awareness and determination to make that film.

Entrepreneurial Spirit

Fr. Kieser was well known in Hollywood among creative talent and industry executives, not only because of his productions, but because he found a way to get on the phone and talk to them. He called development directors asking them to hear his pitch for a new TV series. He called actors to get them to commit to doing an *Insight* episode between their other projects. He called writers to tell them to donate their Humanitas Prize money, or to give of their time by speaking to his writers' workshop. They didn't always want to hear from him!

Fr. Bud once confided to me that when he first started in the business, he would be shaking in his boots when he had to make those calls. He got over it because of the conviction that he wasn't asking for himself—he was asking for God. This ultimately was the source of his persistence. As he states in his autobiography about the making of *Romero*: "No matter how long it took, no matter how many times we were turned down, no matter how discouraging it got, we had to make this movie."[10] That's because he wasn't doing it for himself.

The Ocean and the Mountain

St. Augustine once made a distinction between "the book of revelation" (the Scriptures) and "the book of creation" (nature). Both, he said, are ways God chooses to communicate to human beings. Fr. Bud opened up the book of creation and found the Creator waiting for him. His experiences of nature were a source of prayer and spiritual insight.

Everyone who knew Fr. Bud during his days at the Paulist Productions office in Pacific Palisades, California, knew of his daily swims in the ocean. The building, donated by one of his supporters, sat on Pacific Coast Highway, with stunning views of the Santa Monica Bay. Every day he would take time away from the stresses of work, walk across the busy highway via a pedestrian bridge, and wade into the sea. Fr. Bud, with his large and towering six-foot-seven-inch frame, often seemed weighted down by gravity on land. In the water, he could "let go" physically, emotionally, and spiritually. It was more than just exercise for him; it was contemplation. The ocean was an image of the God beyond his imagining, who gave birth to him, enveloped him in love, lifted him up, and guided his journey.

Another vivid example of his spiritual connection to nature emerges in a passage from his autobiography. Describing an experience while skiing at Palisades Tahoe, he writes of how the mountain represented to him both a primitive struggle of assent, and an exhilarating surrender, "hurtling downhill at colossal speed, the wind tearing at my face."[11] This, too, was for him a launchpad for contemplation. He describes how the ecstasy of the mountain prepared him for an inner stillness that propelled him beyond words or concepts. It brought him to an intimate encounter with the One he calls "an incomprehensible mystery, a bottomless abyss, an infinite horizon, the ground of all being, the realest of the real."

Ultimately, it was Fr. Bud's faith that produced *Insight*. Each episode, and every film he produced afterward, was a response to God's love, a love that awakened his soul, captured his imagination, and inspired his sense of justice. He challenged the creative community in Hollywood to both entertain and enrich their audiences. He sought to serve others as a producer, but as a priest first. And like his patron, St. Paul, he could finally say: *"I have fought the good fight, I have finished the race, I have kept the faith."* (2 Tim 4:7)

Appendix
The Writers and Directors

It is easy to see how *Insight* brought together exceptional acting talent in a unique way. We recognize other creative collaborators whose work formed and enriched this distinctive series. Many made significant contributions to television and film history.[12]

Writers

Bernard Abbene Professor and Chair in the Communication Arts Department of Loyola Marymount University in Los Angeles. Known for his immensely popular "Tuesday Night at the Movies" class and for bringing industry professionals to speak on campus.

Josef Anderson Known for work on *ABC Afterschool Specials*, and the series *Call to Glory* and *Sliders*.

Theodore Apstein Numerous credits include *Ben Casey*, *Dr. Kildare*, *The FBI*, and *Kung Fu*.

John D. F. Black Numerous credits include *Room 222*, *Hawaii Five-O*, *Charlie's Angeles*, and *Star Trek: The Next Generation*.

William Peter Blatty Achieved renown as the author of *The Exorcist*. Wrote and directed *The Exorcist III*.

John Bloch Numerous credits include *The Man from U.N.C.L.E.*, *The Sixth Sense*, and *Police Woman*.

Walter Bodlander Played himself in a Television movie *Things We Did Last Summer*.

Richard Breen Numerous credits include screenplays for the films *Dragnet*, *State Fair*, and *PT 109*.

Thomas Caramagno An educator and writer, known for his books *Flight of the Mind*, *It Isn't Just Me, Is It?*, and *Irreconcilable Differences?*

Otis Carney Known for *Zane Gray Theatre* and *The Monroes*. Also, an author of many books, both fiction and non-fiction, including *Love at First Flight*, *When the Bough Breaks*, and *New Lease on Life*.

Michael Crichton Enjoyed an illustrious career writing screenplays for films and series based on his novels including *Jurassic Park*, *Westworld*, and *The Andromeda Strain*. Also, the creator and executive producer of the successful television series *ER*.

Maureen Daly Credits include *Mannix* and *Police Surgeon*.

William Donnelly Writer as well as a script consultant for *Insight*.

Pamela Douglas Credits include *Trapper John, M.D.*, *Ghostwriter*, and *CBS Schoolbreak Specials*.

John T. Dugan Numerous credits include *Bonanza*, *Star Trek: The Original Series*, *Adam-12*, *Columbo*, and *Little House on the Prairie*.

Ben Elisco Wrote for *WKRP in Cincinnati*.

John Fante Wrote the screenplays for the films *Walk on the Wild Side*, *The Reluctant Saint*, and *Full of Life*, based on his own novel.

John Farrell Also worked as an associate producer on *Insight*.

Howard Fast (as E.V. Cunningham) An accomplished novelist whose work earned several television adaptations, including *April Morning, Freedom Road,* and *The Crossing.* The film adaptation of his novel *Spartacus* won four Oscars.

David C. Field Known for the films *Amazing Grace and Chuck, Passion of Mind,* and the TV movie *Invisible Child.*

Richard Fielder Numerous credits include *The Virginian, The Waltons, Gunsmoke, Born Free,* and *Marcus Welby, M.D.*

John Figueroa Known for the TV series *Switch.*

Harry Julian Fink Numerous credits include screenplays for the films *Major Dundee* and *Magnum Force.*

Dehl Franke aka **Dehl Berti** Became a character actor in numerous television series, including *The Adventures of Rin Tin Tin, Bat Masterson, The Six Million Dollar Man,* and *Saved by the Bell.*

John Furia, Jr. Numerous credits include *Bonanza, The Twilight Zone,* and *The Waltons.* Developed the series *Hotel* for television. Known for the film *The Singing Nun.* Served as President of the Writers Guild of America and later as the Director of the Film Writing Program at USC.

Hank Garson Numerous credits include *The Danny Thomas Show, The Lucy Show, My Three Sons,* and *Family Affair.*

Michael Gleason Numerous credits include *Payton Place, McCloud, Remington Steele,* and *Diagnosis Murder.*

Robert Goodwin Numerous credits include *Julia, Love American Style, Here Come the Brides,* and *All in the Family.*

Jack Hanrahan Numerous credits include *Get Smart, Laugh-In,* and the *Love Boat.* Won the 1967 Emmy for Outstanding Writing Achievement in Music or Variety for *Rowan and Martin's Laugh-In.*

Charlie Hauck Numerous credits include *M*A*S*H, Maude, Valerie, Home Improvement*, and *Frasier*.

Michael Alan Humm Known for *Simon and Simon*.

David Karp Numerous credits include *Playhouse 90, The Defenders*, and *Nero Wolf*. Developed the television series *Garrison's Gorillas*.

Christopher Keane Known for the series *The Huntress* and the TV movie *Dangerous Company*.

John T. Kelly Known for *The Millionaire, Dr. Kildare*, and *Alfred Hitchcock Presents*.

Michael Jay Klassman Known for *Insight*.

Harvey Learner Known for work in the camera and lighting departments for the film *Say Yes*, and the TV movie *The Crown of Bogg*.

John Meredyth Lucas As a writer, known for *Zorro, Ben Casey, Star Trek: The Original Series, Mannix*, and *The Six Million Dollar Man*. Director and/or Producer for numerous shows as well, including *The Fugitive, Night Gallery, Police Surgeon*, and *Star Trek*. Nominated for two Emmys for Outstanding Achievement in Religious Programming for *Insight*.

John McGreevey Numerous credits include *Lassie, The Farmer's Daughter, Hazel, Gidget, The Flying Nun, The Doris Day Show, Mayberry R.F.D.*, and *Ironside*.

Jim McGinn Known for the series *Julia* and the TV movie *Nadia*.

William P. McGivern Numerous credits include *Slattery's People, O'Hara, U.S. Treasury*, and *Kojak*.

Carol Evan McKeand Known for *The Waltons, Family*, and *7th Heaven*. Created the series *The Family Tree*.

James M. Miller Numerous credits include *12 O'Clock High*, *Judd for the Defense*, *The Streets of San Francisco*, and *Knight Rider*.

David Moessinger Numerous credits include *Combat!*, *Mission: Impossible*, *Cannon*, *Police Woman*, *Quincy M.E.*, and *Murder She Wrote*. Director and/or Producer on many series including *Serpico*, *Knots Landing*, *Father Dowling Mysteries*, and *Walker, Texas Ranger*.

James E. Moser aka **Jim Moser** Numerous credits include *Medic*, *Dragnet*, *Ben Casey*, and *Doctors' Hospital*.

Donald Munson Known for *Insight*.

E. Jack Neuman Numerous credits include *The Untouchables* and *The Twilight Zone*. Developed the series *Petrocelli* and *Police Story* for television.

Edmund H. North Known for his film screenplays including *Young Man with a Horn*, *The Day the Earth Stood Still*, and *Patton*.

Lan O'Kun Numerous credits include *The Shari Lewis Show*, *Apple's Way*, *The Love Boat*, and *Highway to Heaven*.

Barry Oringer Numerous credits include *I Spy*, *Medical Center*, and *Barnaby Jones*. With John Furia, Jr., developed the television series *Hotel*.

Gilbert Ralston Numerous credits include *Naked City*, *Ben Casey*, *The Big Valley*, and *Gentle Ben*. Also known for screenplays for the films *Willard* and *Ben*.

Louis Robinson Known for *Insight*.

B.W. Sandefur Numerous credits include *It Takes a Thief*, *Charlie's Angles*, *Little House on the Prairie*, and *The New Mike Hammer*.

Rod Serling A distinguished voice in early television. Created and produced *The Twilight Zone*. Other television credits include *Playhouse 90*, *Armchair Theatre*, and *Night Gallery*. Also known for writing the teleplay for *Requiem for a Heavyweight* and the screenplay for the original *Planet of the Apes*.

Korby Siamis Numerous credits include *Benson. Suddenly Susan, Kate and Allie*, and *Murphy Brown*. As a Producer of *Murphy Brown*, won two Emmys for Outstanding Comedy Series. Also, a producer on *The Middle*.

Richard Alan Simmons Credits include *The Dick Powell Theatre* as well as many TV movies. Developed the series *Mrs. Columbo*. Known for the screenplay for the film *Juggernaut*.

Carol Sobieski aka **Carol O'Brien** Numerous credits include *Peyton Place*, and screenplays for the films *Annie* and *Fried Green Tomatoes*.

Adele Strassfield Known for *The Twilight Zone* and *Gilligan's Island*.

J.S. Sugarhill Known for *Insight*.

Terrance Sweeney Known for producing *Bhopal: A Prayer for Rain* and *The Juggler of Notre Dame*.

Leon Tokatyan Numerous credits include *The Asphalt Jungle, The Outcasts, Lou Grant*, and *Double Dare*.

Diana Bell Tokatyan Known for *Here's Boomer* and *For Love and Honor*.

David H. Vowell Numerous credits include *Mod Squad, O'Hara, U.S. Treasury*, and *Adam-12*.

E. Sarsfield Waters aka **Ed Waters** Numerous credits include *The F.B.I., Baretta, T.J. Hooker*, and *Jake and the Fatman*. Developed the television series *Bronk*.

Stanford Whitmore Numerous credits include *Johnny Staccato, The Fugitive, Night Gallery*, and *The Hitchhiker*.

Lydia Wiggins Known for *Insight*.

John Sacret Young Accomplished writer, director and producer on numerous series and TV movies. Known for his work on *The Fitzpatricks, China Beach, The West Wing,* and *Firefly Lane*.

John Zodrow Known for TV movies *Man Against the Mob* and *Kate Bliss and the Ticker Tape Kid*.

David Zodrow Known for *Insight*.

Directors

Richard C. Bennett Credits include *Alias Smith and Jones, Harry O, Emergency!,* and a number of *ABC Afterschool Specials*.

Richard Beymer Directed several documentaries. Numerous television acting credits include *Twin Peaks, Star Trek: Deep Space Nine, Paper Dolls,* and *Murder She Wrote*. Best known for his starring film role in *West Side Story*.

Robert Butler Numerous credits include *The Untouchables, Hogan's Heroes, Batman,* and *Remington Steele*. Won Emmys for Outstanding Directing in a Drama Series for *Hill Street Blues* and *The Blue Knight*. Winner of Lifetime Achievement Award from the Directors Guild of America in 2015.

Lamar Caselli Known for the TV series *Death Valley Days*.

Curt Conway Known for *Starlight Theatre* and *Crime Photographer*. As an actor, credits include *Peyton Place, The Rookies,* and *The Odd Couple*.

Hal Cooper Accomplished Writer, Producer and Director. Directing credits include *The Dick Van Dyck Show, I Dream of Jeannie, The Doris Day Show, Bridget Loves Bernie,* and *Gimme a Break!*

Mike Cozzi Known for *Insight.*

Marc Daniels Numerous credits include *I Love Lucy, Gunsmoke, Star Trek: The Original Series, The Doris Day Show,* and *Private Benjamin.*

Linda Day Numerous credits include *Newhart, St. Elsewhere, Who's the Boss?, Dallas,* and *Mad About You.*

Charles S. Dubin Numerous credits include *Hawaii Five-O, Lou Grant, M*A*S*H, Trapper John, M.D.* and *Father Dowling Mysteries.*

Mel Ferber Numerous credits include *McMillan and Wife, The Mary Tyler Moore Show, Happy Days, Alice,* and *Diff'rent Strokes.*

Joe Gannon Directing, writing and producing credits include *In the Heat of the Night, Gloria, Archie Bunker's Place,* and *Law & Order.*

Murray Golden Numerous credits include *Death Valley Days, Burke's Law, Batman, The Flying Nun,* and *Medical Center.*

Harvey Hart Directing, writing and producing credits include *Quest, Folio, Peyton Place,* and *Spenser: For Hire.*

Arthur Hiller Numerous television credits include *Perry Mason, The Rifleman, Naked City, and Route 66.* Best known for his films, including *The Out of Towners, Love Story, Plaza Suite, The Hospital, Man of La Mancha,* and *Silver Streak.* Won the Jean Hersholt Humanitarian Award at the 2002 Oscars.

Bill Hobin Directing and producing credits include *The Red Skelton Hour, Your Show of Shows, The Judy Garland Show, Welcome Back Kotter,* and *Three's Company.*

Leonard Horn Numerous credits include *Stoney Burke, The Outer Limits, Voyage to the Bottom of the Sea,* and *It Takes A Thief.*

Lamont Johnson Numerous credits include *Have Gun – Will Travel, The Law and Mr. Jones,* and *The Twilight Zone.* Known for the TV Miniseries *Lincoln* and *The Kennedys of Massachusetts.*

Jim Johnson Credits include *The Nat King Cole Show.*

Michael J. Kane Credits include *The Linkletter Show, Quincey M.E.,* and *Hardcastle and McCormick.*

Herb Kenwith Credits include *Here's Lucy, Good Times,* and *One Day at a Time.*

Buzz Kulik Numerous credits include *Gunsmoke, Playhouse 90, The Defenders,* and the TV Miniseries *George Washington.* Won the 1972 Directors Guild of America Award for Outstanding Directorial Achievement in Movies for Television for *Brian's Song.*

Gene Law Credits include *Here's Hollywood* and *Where the Action Is.*

J.D. Lobue Numerous credits include *Soap, It's a Living, Soul Train, Herman's Head,* and *Dharma and Greg.*

Norman Lloyd Directing, producing and acting credits include *Tales of the Unexpected, The Name of the Game,* and *St. Elsewhere.* Known for his role in *Dead Poets Society.*

John Meredyth Lucas *See* Writers

Will MacKenzie Numerous credits include *Bosom Buddies, Family Ties, Major Dad, Everybody Loves Raymond,* and *Scrubs.*

Delbert Mann Numerous television credits include *The Philco Playhouse, Goodyear Playhouse,* and *Omnibus.* Known for his theatrical films, including *Lover Come Back, Desire Under the Elms, That*

Touch of Mink, and *Kidnapped.* Won the Oscar for Best Director for *Marty.* Received the Directors Guild of America Honorary Life Member Award in 2002.

Alex March Numerous credits include *Ben Casey, The Long Hot Summer, N.Y.P.D.,* and *Barney Miller.*

Sherman Marks Numerous credits include *General Electric Theatre, Mike Hammer, Petticoat Junction,* and *The Man from U.N.C.L.E.*

David O. McDearmon Numerous credits include *The Twilight Zone, The Aquanauts, Bewitched,* and *Gilligan's Island.*

John Newland Numerous credits include *The Loretta Young Show, Bachelor Father, Daniel Boone, The Young Lawyers,* and *Wonder Woman.*

Paul Nickell Known for *Insight.*

John Peyser Numerous credits include *The Frank Sinatra Show, Studio One, The Lloyd Bridges Show, Rat Patrol,* and *Switch.*

Daniel Petrie Numerous credits include *The Billy Rose Show, Armstrong Circle Theatre, East Side/West Side,* and the TV movie *Eleanor and Franklin: The White House Years.* Known for his theatrical films *Lifeguard, Resurrection,* and *Fort Apache the Bronx.*

Russ Petranto Credits include *Sanford and Son, CPO Sharkey, Too Close for Comfort,* and *She's the Sheriff.*

Ted Post Numerous credits include *Wagon Train, Rawhide,* and *Cagney and Lacey.* Known for his theatrical films *Beneath the Planet of the Apes, The Harrad Experiment,* and *Go Tell the Spartans.*

Mike Rhodes Numerous credits include *A Year in the Life, China Beach, Christy,* and *Beverly Hills 90210.* Produced a number of Paulist Productions TV movies and films, including *The Fourth Wise-*

man and *We Are the Children*. Directed Fr. Kieser's second feature film *Entertaining Angels: The Dorothy Day Story*.

John Rich Numerous credits include *I Married Joan, Our Miss Brooks, Bat Masterson, The Dick Van Dyke Show, Gomer Pyle: USMC,* and *All in the Family*.

Seymour Robbie Numerous credits include *The Green Hornet, F-Troop, The Magical World of Disney, The Streets of San Francisco, Barnaby Jones,* and *Ellery Queen*.

Sutton Roley Numerous credits include *77 Sunset Strip, Lost in Space, S.W.A.T., Vega$, Airwolf,* and *Starsky and Hutch*.

Jay Sandrich Numerous credits include *The Danny Thomas Show, Get Smart, The Ghost and Mrs. Muir, Nanny and the Professor, The Odd Couple, Laverne and Shirley, The Mary Tyler Moore Show, Rhoda, Phyllis,* and *Night Court*.

Ralph Senensky Numerous credits include *The Fugitive, Star Trek: The Original Series, The Courtship of Eddie's Father, The Partridge Family, Eight Is Enough, The Waltons, Dynasty, Hart to Hart,* and *Paper Dolls*.

Jack Shea Numerous credits include *The Jerry Lewis Show, The Bob Hope Show, Death Valley Days, The Jeffersons, Silver Spoons, Designing Women,* and *Growing Pains*. Won the Directors Guild of America's Robert B. Aldrich Achievement Award in 1992.

James Sheldon Numerous credits include *The Millionaire, The Donna Reed Show, The Patty Duke Show, My Three Sons, Room 222, Love American Style, The Love Boat,* and *The Dukes of Hazzard*.

Paul Stanley Numerous credits include *Appointment with Adventure, Goodyear Playhouse, Combat!, Tarzan, The Time Tunnel, Then Came Bronson, Charlie's Angels, Lou Grant,* and *The Fall Guy*.

Phil Thorton Known for *Insight*.

Nicholas Webster Credits include *The Twentieth Century, Braken's World*, and *In Search of*. Known for the film *Santa Claus Conquers the Martians*.

Gordon Wiles Credits include *Here's Eddie, Rowan and Martin's Laugh-In, The Bobby Darin Show,* and *Land of the Lost*.

Joel Zwick Numerous credits include *Mork and Mindy, Joanie Loves Chachi, Webster, Full House,* and *Girl Meets World*. Known for his theatrical films *My Big Fat Greek Wedding, Fat Albert,* and *Elvis Has Left the Building*.

Bibliography

"A Little Insight: Interview with Paulist Productions' Father Ellwood Kieser," *Emmy*, Academy of Television Arts and Sciences, North Hollywood, Vol.5 (2), March 1, 1983.

Abernethy, Bob, "Father Ellwood 'Bud' Kieser," *Religion and Ethics Newsweekly*, July 9, 1999. www.pbs.org/wnet/religionandethics/1999/07/09/july-9-1999-father-ellwood-bud-kieser/15402/

Boxall, Bettina, "Priest, TV Producer Ellwood Kiser Dies," *Los Angeles Times*, Sept. 18, 2000.

Gould, Jack, "TV: Paulist Fathers Face Real Issues," *New York Times*, June 9, 1969.

"'Insight' Series Achieves Primetime Status on May 3," *Hollywood Reporter*, April 30, 1965.

Kieser, Ellwood E., *Hollywood Priest: A Spiritual Struggle*, Doubleday, New York, 1991.

Kieser, Ellwood, "TV Could Nourish Minds and Hearts," *Time*, Sept.14, 1992.

Mankin, Eric, "The Producer Priest Gets a Shot at Primetime," *Los Angeles Herald Examiner*, Nov. 24, 1984.

Margulies, Lee, "TV Reviews: Previewing the New Season," *Los Angeles Times*, Sept. 14, 1978.

Nastasi, Alison, "Film Recalls the 'Hollywood Priest' Who Disrupted the Entertainment Industry," *Angelus News*, Oct 13, 2021. www.

angelusnews.com/arts-culture/film-recalls-the-hollywood-priest-who-disrupted-the-entertainment-industry/

Ornstein, Bill, "Father Kieser's 'Insight' Show Now Beamed Over 195 Stations," *Hollywood Reporter*, July 27, 1966.

Quigley, Mark, "Between Sign-Off Films and Test Patterns: Insight at UCLA," *The Moving Image*, University of Minnesota Press, Volume 9, Number 1, Spring 2009.

Sachs, Ben, "William Shatner Wrestles with His Soul at 4 AM, and This Priest Has It on Videotape," *Bleader, The Chicago Reader*, Nov. 6, 2014.

Smith, Cecil, "'Insight' Calls God to Account," *Los Angeles Times*, Nov. 27, 1980.

"Television Review: 'All Out,'" *Variety*, July 16, 1976.

"The Interviews," Television Academy Foundation, www.interviews.televisionacademy.com, n.d.

Vils, Ursula, "Priest, Producer, and 'Half a Ham,'" *Los Angeles Times*, April 16, 1984.

Weinraub, Bernard, "Rev. Ellwood Kieser, Priest and Film Producer, Dies at 71," *New York Times*, Sept. 20, 2000.

Notes

1. Kieser, Ellwood E., *Hollywood Priest: A Spiritual Struggle*, Doubleday, New York, 1991, pp. 235-236.

2. Kieser, p. 237.

3. Paulist Productions, "Insight Powered by Paulist Productions," *YouTube*, www.youtube.com/c/InsightPaulistProductions

4. Weinraub, Bernard, "Rev. Ellwood Kieser, Priest and Film Producer, Dies at 71," *New York Times*, Sept. 20, 2000, p. 23.

5. Jamie Farr Interview, Television Academy Foundation, interviewed by Nancy Harrington on Dec. 15, 2011. Visit TelevisionAcademy.com/interviews for more information.

6. Jack Shea Interview, Television Academy Foundation, Interviewed by Jennifer Howard on Dec. 9, 2002. Visit TelevisionAcademy.com/interviews for more information.

7. Kieser, p.238.

8. "Television Review: 'All Out,'" *Variety*, July 16, 1976.

9. Patty Duke Interview, Television Academy Foundation, interviewed by Stephen J. Abramson on Dec. 8, 2013. Visit TelevisionAcademy.com/interviews for more information.

10. Kieser, p.14.

11. Kieser, p.328.

12. Most information in the Appendix has been retrieved from the Internet Movie Database, www.imdb.com

Index

34th Hour, The 60, 63, 64, 183

Abbene, Bernard 49, 188
Abbott, Philip 43, 48, 124
Ackerman, Bettye 17
Ackerman, Leslie 130, 131
Acosta, Carmelita 22
Adams, Julie 35
Addy, Wesley 57
Adele Strassfield 43, 193
Adrian, Nancy 125
Agitator, The 20
Aidman, Charles 40
Albertson, Jack 57, 58, 73, 91, 109, 110
Albertson, Moria 110
Alcalde, Mario 74, 75
Aletter, Frank 98, 104, 114, 123
Alice, Mary 130
All Out 116, 124
All the Little Plumes of Pain 59
All the Things I've Never Liked 66
Alleluia Kid, The 135, 138
Allen, Elizabeth 139
Allen, Mark 53
Allen, Raymond 125
Almaraz, Esther 66
Ambriz, Domingo 162
Amos, John 185
And the Walls Came Tumbling Down 109, 110
Anderson Jr., Michael 131
Anderson, Barbara 54
Anderson, Herbert 39
Anderson, John 176
Anderson, Josef 167, 168, 173, 174, 188
Andrews, C.S.P., Eric vii
Andrews, Edward 48, 87, 105, 117, 165
Androsky, Carol 166
Angarola, Richard 56
Angelini, Marina 165
Aniano, Martha 110
Antonio, Jim 101, 170
Antonio, Lou 64, 111
Apparcel, C.S.P., Gregory vii
Aquinas, St. Thomas 20
Arkin, Alan 180
Arngrim, Stefan 79
Arnstein's Miracle 140
Arquette, Rosanna 177
Ashley, Edward 64
Ashley, Elizabeth 89
Askin, Leon 177
Asner, Ed 1, 51, 62, 69, 82, 87, 93, 94, 141
Astin, John 94, 95, 103, 107, 110, 116, 125, 133, 146
Atkinson, Beverley Hope 125
Attention Must Be Paid 103
Atwater, Barry 47, 87
Atwater, Edith 126
Aubrey, Skye 99
Aubuchon, Jacques 31, 44
Augustine, St. 43, 186

Avery, Brian 89
Avila, Christine 168, 169, 177
Ayres, John 12, 13

Baer, Parley 151
Bailey, David 93, 115, 118
Baker, Diane 49, 94, 95
Bakewell, William 35
Bal, Jeanne 66
Baldavin, Barbara 41, 50
Balding, Rebecca 150
Ballad of Alma Gerlayne, The 64
Baltimore, Lord 12
Bang, Joy 90
Banks, Ernie 140
Bannon, Jack 157
Bara, Fausto 168
Baral, Eileen 87
Barash, Olivia 176
Bard, Katherine 54
Barry, Patricia 40, 60, 86, 93, 103, 122
Barton, Dan 57
Barty, Billy 80
Bassett, William 65
Batanides, Arthur 49
Baur, Elizabeth 66
Baxter, Meredith 90
Beckman, Henry 25, 32, 36, 47, 72
Beelzebub and the Bolsheviks 10, 11
Beggs, James 45
Begley, Jr., Ed 115, 119, 176
Begley, Ed 20, 74
Beir, Fred 79
Belasco, Leon 103, 140
Belfast: Black on Green 142
Belford, Christine 112, 138, 142, 147, 161, 167,
Bellarmine, St. Robert 20

Bellwood, Pamela 124
Benedict, Steve 128
Benjamin, Richard 157
Bennett, Maura 84
Bennett, Richard 25, 37, 38, 41, 43, 48, 49, 55, 82, 84, 85, 91, 94, 98, 99, 105, 106, 109, 114, 115, 118, 119, 122, 123, 125, 126, 127, 130, 134, 139, 157, 159, 171, 194
Benson, Lucille 140
Beregi, Oscar 103
Bergan, Judith-Marie 176
Berlinger, Warren 150
Bernardi, Herschel 16
Bernath, Shari 107
Berti, Dehl 22, 26, 190
Bertoya, Paul 76
Besch, Bibi 162
Bethune, Ivy 26
Bettger, Lyle 53
Betz, Carl 83, 89, 95
Beymer, Richard 121, 154, 155, 194
Bieri, Ramon 122, 157
Bill, Tony 71
Binns, Edward 34, 63, 83
Bird on the Mast, The 85, 91, 92
Birt, Rock 151
Bissell, Whit 74
Bixby, Bill 69, 89
Black, John D. F. 33, 40, 58, 188
Blatty, William Peter 1, 59, 65, 116, 122, 188
Blind Man's Bluff 129
Bloch, John 59, 62, 71, 189
Bloch, Tim 104
Bloodstrike 104
Blyth, Ann 12
Bochner, Lloyd 44, 55, 56, 68, 70
Bodlander, Walter 47, 189

Boles, Bibi 47
Bosley, Tom 119
Boss Toad 28
Bourbon in Suburbia 79
Bowen, Candace 160
Bower, Antoinette 67
Box for Mr. Lipton, A 92, 93
Boy and the Bomb, The 19
Bradbury, Lane 85
Bradshaw, Booker 69, 71, 95
Brandon, Michael 89, 130
Brandt, Martin 22
Braun, Shony 167, 168
Breakthrough 17
Breen, Richard 9, 25, 33, 38, 42, 48, 189
Brennan, Eileen 116
Breslin, Patricia 22
Brewster, William 12
Bridges, Beau 1, 43, 62, 69, 76, 134
Bridges, Jeff 1, 84
Brocco, Peter 103, 140
Brooke, Walter 36, 44, 63, 99, 104, 136, 142, 147,
Brooks, Albert 82
Brooks, Geraldine 36, 45, 68
Brooks, Martin 49
Brothers in the Dark 31
Brown, Barry 126, 131
Brown, Lew 12, 161
Brown, Susan 131
Browne, Roscoe Lee 65, 66
Brubaker, Robert 40, 47
Brunetti, Augustina 43
Bryant, Joshua 131, 165
Buchanan High 179
Bulifant, Joyce 97
Bull, Richard 41, 67
Bundy, Brooke 43, 105, 127

Burghoff, Gary 89, 119, 120
Burkley, Dennis 99
Burnett, Carol 1, 141
Burnham, Terry 51, 52
Burns, Michael 57, 82, 84, 90, 95
Burrell, Jan 40
Burton, Normann 146
Burton, Wendell 112, 113, 127
Butler, Robert 1, 45, 54, 97, 98, 160, 194
Butterfly 173, 177

Cahill, Barry 58, 99
Callahan, James 32, 157, 159
Calomee, Gloria 29
Campanella, Joseph 55, 56, 64, 69
Campos, Rafael 43
Capital Cities 179
Capitalist, The 22, 23
Caramagno, Thomas C. 68, 69, 81, 86, 87, 89, 189
Cardi, Pat 30, 49, 62
Carey, MacDonald 13
Carey, Phil 11
Cargoes 151, 152
Carl, Kitty 106
Carlin, Lynn 109, 121, 130, 131, 139
Carmel, Roger C. 74
Carney, Otis 9, 189
Carr, Darlene 144
Carr, Paul 51, 67, 79
Carroll, Leo G. 17
Carson, John David 119, 120
Carter, Jack 117, 127
Cary, Christopher 76
Caselli, Lamar 34, 41, 47, 194
Casey, Chic 91
Cassidy, Joanna 154
Cassidy, Ted 58

Celebration in Fresh Powder 107
Charlie, You Made the Night Too Long 72, 73
Chastain, Don 64
Checco, Al 79
Checkmate 150
Chew, Sam 121, 169, 171
Chiles, Linden 72
Chipper 118
Christ, Caesar, Conscience 13
Christian Marriage 8
Christmas 2025 135, 139
Christopher, Bill 94
Cianelli, Eduardo 10, 17
Clark, Candace 107
Clark, Dort 47
Clark, Mae 53
Clarke, Angela 109, 140
Clayton, Jan 87, 161
Clearing House, The 176
Clown of Freedom, The 108, 113, 114
Cobb, Julie 167
Coffee House, The 47
Coit, Stephen 37
Colbin, Rod 129
Cole, Norman 108
Colicos, John 126
Colley, Don Pedro 125
Collins, Gary 99, 100, 105, 133
Collins, Jeanne 63
Collins, Russell 38
Coming of the Clone 105
Compos, Rafael 89
Confrontation 83
Connelly, Joseph E. vii, 6, 8, 9, 13, 15
Connolly, Chris 77
Conried, Hans 12
Consider the Zebra 74, 75
Conspirator, The 18
Contreras, Roberto 89, 106
Conversation with Christ 8
Conway, Curt 66, 195
Conwell, Carolyn 47
Cook, Elisha 168
Cooley, Isabel 125
Cooper, Hal 1, 27, 35, 42, 48, 50, 65, 68, 77, 85, 87, 96, 102, 122, 129, 137, 151, 153, 195
Cooper, Jeanne 76, 136
Cord, Alex 97
Corden, Henry 25, 48, 51
Corey, Jeff 48
Cornthwaite, Robert 52
Cort, Bud 166
Costello, Anthony 85, 91, 105, 113, 138, 149, 170
Costello, Mariclare 133
Cox, Ronny 134
Cozzi, Mike 6, 8, 14, 195
Crain, Jeanne 18
Crane, Norma 51
Crane, Susan 54
Crawford, Jr., Robert 59
Crichton, Michael 1, 85, 88, 92, 97, 108, 111, 189
Crier, Jennifer 41
Crime of Innocence, The 108, 109
Cromwell, James 135, 139
Cross in the Crisis 14
Cross of Russia 30
Crowley, Pat 26
Crunch on Spruce Street 85, 86
Cry of Terror 79, 80
Cullen, William-Kirby 130
Culp, Robert 18
Cum Laude, Come Lonely 133
Curtwright, Jorja 18

Dalton, Audrey 11, 12, 32
Daly, Maureen 65, 69, 189
Dangerous Airs of Amy Clark 75, 77, 78
Daniels, Marc 38, 45, 63, 74, 93, 103, 108, 112, 116, 130, 142, 148, 151, 167, 195
Daniels, William 121
Danson, Ted 180
Darrow, Henry 106
DaSilva, Howard 140
David, Brad 81
David, Clifford 146
Davidson, Davey 54, 55
Davis, Ann B. 67
Davis, Bette x
Davison, Bruce 76, 86, 100, 150
Davison, Davey 94, 115, 130, 157
Day Everything Went Wrong, The 174, 175
Day God Died, The 70, 71
Day, Gerry 33, 35, 40
Day, Linda 161, 195
Dayton, June 35, 57, 62
de Foucauld, St. Charles 26
de Santis, Joe 24, 30
de Vargas, Val 106
de Wilde, Brandon 83
de Winter, Johanna 109
Death of Simon Jackson, The 68, 71, 72
Death of Superman, The 85
Death of the Elephant 92, 94, 95
Decision to Love, A 165, 166
DeCoy, Robert 29, 50
DeGruy, Jr., Oscar 120
Dehner, John 33, 41, 81
Demyan, Lincoln 45
Denbeaux, Jacques 37, 38

Dennis, John 65
Dern, Lara 179
des Lunde, Robert 48
Desiderio, C.S.P., Frank vii, xi
Deuel, Geoffrey 65
Devane, William 171, 172
Devargus, Val 74
Devon, Laura 32
Dexter, Alan 112
Deyer, Gloria Lynn 137
DeYoung, Cliff 116, 125, 128
Diary of a Beatnik 25
Diaz, Edith 89, 117, 165
Diaz, Maria 56
Dierking, Sharon 105
Dillard, Mimi 48
Dillman, Bradford 48
Dillon, Melinda 1, 163, 164, 165, 166, 167, 168, 177
Dixon, Ivan xii, 29
Dixon, Patti 168
Dobbins, Bennie 110
Dobkin, Lawrence 26, 32
Dog That Bit You, The 34, 35
Domasin, Larry 24
Domino Effect, The 161, 162
Don't Elbow Me Off the Earth 42
Don't Let Me Catch You Praying 42, 48
Donahue, Elinor 139
Donnelly, William 22, 189
Doohan, James 140
Dooley, Tom 10
Doqui, Robert 71, 100, 125, 142, 161
Doucette, John 47
Douglas, Pamela 173, 177, 189
Downs, Frederic 37
Doyle, Peggy 105, 106, 114, 118, 124, 126, 138, 144

Doyle, Robert 57, 59, 79
Driscoll, Don 10, 11, 12, 13, 14
Dry Commitment, A 56
Dubbins, Don 69, 89
Dubin, Charles S. 101, 195
Duel, Peter 82, 83
Duff, Howard 74, 91
Dugan, John T. 25, 30, 55, 83, 105, 117, 127, 135, 189
Dugdale, Charles 36
Duggan, Andrew 76, 114, 149
Duggan, Bob 47, 48, 53, 62, 110, 133
Duggan, John T. 42, 48, 50, 74, 116
Duggan, Robert 37, 105
Duke, Patty 107, 110, 133, 137, 146, 147, 162, 176, 185
Duke, Raymond 146, 155
Dunhill, Peter 47
Dunn, Liam 71
Dunne, Brian 47
Dunne, Irene 10,
Duryea, Peter 87
Dutton's Choice 173, 174
Dysart, Richard 177

Ecce Homo 15
Eddie 108
Edith Stein Story, The 16
Egan, Richard 26, 27
Eilbacher, Cindy 128
Einstein, Dan xi
Elcar, Dana 174
Elder, Ann 49
Elisco, Ben 165, 176, 189
Elizondo, Hector 161
Elkins, Richard 55, 56, 71
Eltinge, Patricia 156
Emhardt, Robert 80
Entertaining Angels: The Dorothy Day Story 180
Erasmus 20
Erdman, Richard 47
Erickson, Leif 47
Estevez, Emilio 153, 159, 179
Eure, Wesley 146
Evans, Richard 49
Every Ninety Seconds 167, 169, 170
Exit Sound 82
Eye of the Camel 106
Eyer, Richard 28, 32

Fabric of Freedom 12
Face of Tyranny, The 11
Faith, A Reason To live, A Reason to Die 8
Fante, John 24, 189
Faracy, Stephanie 165
Farentino, James 41, 147, 154, 162, 163, 164
Farnon, Shannon 49
Farr, Jamie 24, 25
Farrell, John 130, 189
Farrell, Sharon 61, 108, 111
Fast, Howard (E.V. Cunningham) 1, 114, 190
Fat Hands and a Diamond Ring 58, 59
Faulkner, Edward 32
FCC 1, 3
Feinstein, Alan 156, 161
Feldman, Marty 159, 160
Fell, Norman 49, 51
Ferber, Mel 49, 195
Ferrone, Dan 89
Fiddler, The 167, 168
Field, David C. 163, 170, 173, 176, 190
Fielder, John 76

Fielder, Richard 135, 138, 147, 148, 165, 190
Figueroa, John 89, 190
Fink, Harry Julian 37, 47, 52, 190
Fire Within, The 39
Fisher of Men 32
Fisher, Gail 76
Fitzpatrick, Tom 157
Five Without Faces 89
Flawed Magi 142, 146
Fleming, Ed 14
Fluellen, Joel 71, 72, 74, 104
Flynn, Joe 35, 97
Fonda, Peter 49
For Better or for Worse 19
For Love or Money 172
For the Love of Annie 127, 133
Ford, Bishop Frank 14
Forrest, Steve 30, 31, 53
Forsythe, John 18, 47
Fortier, Robert 29
Fourth Wiseman, The 179, 182
Fox, Michael 86
Foxworth, Robert 101, 106
Francis, Anne 79, 102
Francis, Ivor 77, 97, 102
Franciscus, James 123
Franke, Dehl 28, 48, 190
Franken, Steve 76, 80, 127, 134, 140, 143,
Franklin, Pamela 119
Franz, Eduard 16, 39, 45, 46
Freak, The 93, 94
Frederick, Hal 72, 74
Freed, Bert 41, 87
Freeman, Joan 49
Friends 98
Funny Thing Happened on the Way, A 50, 51

Furia, Jr., John vii, 9, 16, 17, 18, 19, 20, 37, 40, 41, 50, 51, 52, 54, 55, 56, 57, 58, 59, 65, 66, 67, 75, 77, 79, 80, 81, 82, 83, 84, 93, 94, 96, 97, 98, 190

Gail, Max 177
Game Room, The 177
Gannon, Joe 161, 195
Garas, Kaz 87, 99
Garcia, Stella 43
Gardenia, Vincent 150, 151
Garland, Beverly 33, 34, 41, 42, 43, 53, 70, 94, 174
Garr, Terri 49
Garson, Hank 9, 190
Gartlan, Niall 161
Garver, Kathy 62
Gautier, Dick 127
Gaviola, Sandy 128
Geer, Ellen 108, 155, 165, 170
Gelman, Larry 143
Gentri, John 47
Georgiade, Nick 77
Gerber, Joan 73
Gerritsen, Lisa 80
Ghetto Trap, The 65
Ghostley, Alice 65
Gibbons, C.S.P., Thomas vii
Gibson, Beau 110
Gilman, Sam 166
Gingold, Dan 15
Girl in Freefall 130, 131
Girl on the Edge of Town, The 179
Glass, Ned 54, 58, 103
Glass, Ron 101
Gleason, Michael 41, 190
Gleason, Regina 35
Glenn, Roy 77

God and the Atheists 10
God in the Dock 151, 155, 156
God's Guerillas 158, 162, 163
Golden, Ginny 106
Golden, Murray 105, 195
Golonka, Arlene 61, 85, 96, 159
Gomez, Panchito 159
Gomez, Thomas 22
Goodbye 157
Goodeve, Grant 136, 172
Goodwin, Robert 68, 71, 190
Gordon, Don 24, 25, 40
Goretti, St. Maria 17
Gorshim, Frank 17
Gossett, Jr., Lou 1, 123
Gould, Harold 58, 65, 66, 148, 149, 102, 133, 150, 151, 153
Gould, Sandra 105
Governor's Mansion, The 47
Graduation Day 99, 100
Grady, Don 91
Graham, Tim 37
Granger, Farley 63
Gray, Coleen 25
Greatest Madness of Them All, The 81
Greening, Judy vii, 157
Gregg, Virginia 65
Gregory, James 43
Grimm, Maria 168
Groom, Sam 139
Gross, Todd 110
Grover, Ed 165
Gulager, Clu 105
Gun for Mandy, A 170, 171

Hackman, Gene 1, 83
Haddon, Laurence 108
Hale, Barbara 71
Halleck, Dan 82
Halop, Florence 96, 174
Hamill, Mark 112
Hamilton, Bernie 53
Hamilton, Kim 41, 50
Hamilton, Lynn 74, 161, 125
Hammer, Don 67
Hampton, James 137
Hang-Up 54
Hanley, Bridget 134
Hanlon, Robert x
Hanrahan, Jack 1, 68, 69, 75, 80, 92, 94, 100, 105, 127, 190
Hanrahan, Jamie 81
Hanrahan, Romarie 105
Happiness 8
Happy Birthday, Marvin 102
Harden, Jr., Ernest 176
Harrington, Pat 28, 128, 129
Harris, Berkeley 38
Harris, Jonathan 96
Harris, Julius 146, 147, 148
Harris, Robert H. 22, 93, 134
Hart, Dolores 18
Hart, Harvey 67, 195
Hartley, Mariette 70, 119
Harty, Patricia 55, 56
Haskell, Peter 69, 155
Haskin, Byron 114
Hastings, Bob 124
Hate Syndrome, The 42, 45, 46
Hauck, Charlie 135, 137, 191
Hausner, Jerry 12, 14
Hayes, Jimmy 30
Haze, Stan 125
He Lived with Us, He Ate with Us, What Else, Dear? 60
Heart of Liberty 12
Hellbound Blues 116, 125

Helm, Anne 16
Henderson, Ty 119, 125
Henning, Bunny 49
Herbert, Pitt 74
Hermit, The 25
Hershey, Barbara 57, 58
Hewitt, Alan 49
Hey, Hey, Billy Rae 75, 84
Hey, Janitor 106
Heyson, Dilart 72
Hickman, Darryl 13
Hickman, Dwayne 61
Hicks, Hilly 76
Higgins, Joe 30, 32, 47, 50
Higgins, Joel 174, 175
High Powder 179
Highest Bidder, The 85, 91
Hiller, Arthur 1, 28, 58, 83, 111, 195
His Feet Don't Stink 128, 129
Hit Man 173, 176
Hobin, Bill 47, 196
Hogan, Bob 119, 130
Hogan, Jack 139
Hogan, Robert 114, 115, 120
Holbrook, Nancy 169
Holdridge, Cheryl 28
Hollahan, C.S.P., Tom vii
Holland, Kristina 112, 113
Holliman, Earl 83
Holm, Celeste 1, 58, 59
Holy Moses 150, 151
Homeier, Skip 25, 31
Horn, Leonard 62, 196
Houser, Jerry 120, 122, 149, 160
Howard, Clint 87, 102
Howard, Ron 119, 160
Howard, Vince 125
Howard, Wendy Smith 177
Hoyt, John 18, 49

Huffman, Rosanna 69
Hull, Cynthia 100
Humanitas Master Writers' Workshops 184
Humanitas Prize 184, 185
Humm, Michael Alan 115, 127, 128, 191
Hundley, Craig 109
Hunger Knows My Name 121
Hunter, Jeff 52, 69
Hunter, Kim 116, 122
Hursey, Sherry 162
Hurst, David 140
Hurst, Gordon 146
Hussey, Ruth 20
Hylands, Scott 151
Hyman, Bob 113

I Want to Die 136
I'm Gonna Be Free 99
Incident on Danker Street 75, 76, 77
Incredible Man, The 119, 120
Invincible Weapon, The 28, 29
IOU My Brother 14
Is Anyone Listening? 142, 144, 183
Is the 11:59 Late This Year? 74

Jackson, Jamie Smith 128, 130, 131
Jackson, Mary 58
Jaeckel, Richard 96, 97
James, Loren 116
Jameson, Joyce 80
Janis, Conrad 169
Jefferson, Thomas 11, 20, 29
Jensen, Karen 96
Jesus B.C. 127, 135
Jesus Experience, The 182
Jesus Song, The 100
Jillian, Ann 17

Johnson, Jim 8, 10, 11, 12, 13, 16, 17, 18, 19, 196
Johnson, Keg 29
Johnson, Lamont 61, 88, 196
Johnson, Sander 113
Juggler of Notre Dame, The 179
Jones, Lindsey 120
Jordan, Richard 172, 173
Jory, Victor 14
Julia, Raul 180
Just Before Eve 144, 145
Justice, Katherine 126
Juvie 130

Kane, Michael J. 24, 196
Karnes, Robert 62
Karp, David 57, 191
Kaye, Celia 59
Kaye, Judy 82
Keane, Christopher 151, 152, 191
Kearney, Carolyn 25
Keen, Noah 84, 99
Keep, Stephan 151, 152, 161, 167
Keith, Brian x, 12, 20, 28, 30, 32, 39, 43, 63
Kellerman, Sally 33, 34
Kelly, Brian 32
Kelly, John T. 28, 52, 191
Kelly, Moira 180
Kelly, Paula 135
Kelman, Rick 43, 107, 115
Kennedy, Richard 20
Kent, Janice 150
Kenwith, Herb 89, 196
Kenyon, Sandy 97, 146
Kerwin, Lance 115, 170, 171
Kid Show, The 30
Killer, The (1963) 17
Killer, The (1972) 92, 97

Kilpatrick, Lincoln 74, 75
King of the Penny Arcade 115
King, Freeman 125
King, Jon 110
Kirkland, Sally 171
Klassman, Michael Jay 128, 191
Kleeb, Helen 54
Klemperer, Werner 18, 22
Kline, Richard 176
Klugman, Jack 1, 22, 30, 143
Kolbe, St. Maximillian 22
Kopell, Bernie 99
Korman, Harvey 85, 86
Kovak, Nancy 72
Kristen, Marta 74
Kulik, Buzz 1, 48, 74, 133, 165, 196

Lacy, Laura 139
Landesberg, Steve 172
Lane, Lola x
Laneuville, Eric 128
Lang, Doreen 16, 81
Lansing, Robert 33, 38, 45, 51, 52, 62, 63, 94
Larch, John 87, 88, 99
Larsen, Debby 52
Last of the Great Male Chauvinists 116, 122
Late Great God, The 60, 67
Launeuville, Eric 124
Law, Gene 26, 196
Leach, Britt 85
Leak, Jennifer 81
Learned, Michael 104
Learner, Harvey 99, 191
Least of My Brothers, The 43
Leave Me Alone, God 167, 172, 173
Leeds, Peter 25, 100
Leighton, Linda 39

Lembeck, Harvey 96, 97
Lenin, Vladimir 12, 19
Lenz, Kay 169
Lenz, Rick 167
Leo XIII, Pope 17
Leonard, Mark 70
Leroy 140
Leslie, Bethel 149
Leslie, Joan 16
Lewis, Sandy 29
Lewis, Sanford 41
Libertini, Richard 177
Lichine, David 8
Lindley, Audra 165
Lindsay, George 85
Lippe, Jonathan 69, 105
Lipton, Robert 71
Little Miseries 165
Lloyd, Norman 1, 176, 196
Lobue, J.D. 140, 163, 172, 196
Locke, John 20
Lockhart, June 166
Locusts Have No King 33, 36, 37
Long Road Home 153
Look Back to the Garden 61
Lopez, Rafael 24
Loren, James 35, 36, 38, 39, 42, 43, 44, 45, 47, 48
Love Song of the Coo Coo Birds 96
Love, Phyllis 37
Lovers, The 28
Lovsky, Celia 17
Lowe, Stanya 67
Lowens, Curt 81
Lucas, Elizabeth 108
Lucas, John Meredyth vii, 21, 27, 33, 38, 43, 51, 60, 61, 62, 63, 64, 65, 68, 69, 70, 71, 72, 73, 74, 79, 85, 86, 87, 88, 89, 90, 91, 95, 96, 99, 100, 101, 102, 103, 104, 105, 106, 107, 108, 109, 110, 111, 112, 113, 114, 116, 117, 118, 119, 120, 121, 122, 123, 124, 125, 126, 127, 128, 129, 130, 131, 133, 134, 135, 139, 144, 154, 191
Lundigan, William 17
Lupino, Ida xii, 91
Lupton, John 109
Lurie, Alan 85, 91, 105, 127, 133, 134, 139, 171
Lynch, Ken 76
Lynn, Janis 115, 125

MacArthur, James 16, 50
MacKenzie, William 169, 176, 196
Macklin, David 62, 63
MacLachlan, Janet 65, 121, 128
Macleod, Murray 101
MacRae, Ellen 66
MacRae, Meredith 62
Macready, George 18
Madam 52
Madison, James 13
Maffeo, Neil T. 48, 49
Malave, Chu Chu 130
Mallory, Carol 169
Malone, Nancy 67
Malooly, Maggie 94
Man from Inner Space, The 116, 123
Man in the Cast Iron Suit 127, 131, 132
Man in the Middle 52, 53
Man of the Year, The 127
Man Who Mugged God, The 147, 148, 149
Man Who Went Blue Sky, The 112, 113

Mandan, Robert 106
Mandley, Lawrence 151
Mann, Delbert 1, 162, 197
Manning, Jack 112, 118
Mantooth, Randolph 159, 160
Manza, Ralph 70
March, Alex 56, 197
Marcus, Sparky 139
Marcuse, Theodore 26
Marks, Sherman 52, 197
Marley, Ben 133
Marley, John 18, 67, 81, 87
Mars, Ken 93, 129
Marsac, Maurice 25
Marshall, William 29, 56
Marta, Lynne 107
Martin, D'urville 49, 61, 65, 125
Martin, Helen 138
Martin, Nan 120, 124, 160
Martinez, A 106, 152, 162
Martyr, The 21
Marx Brothers x
Marx, Karl 12, 19
Masak, Ron 85
Mason, Marlyn 98
Massey, Raymond 1, 14, 17
Matchpoint 167, 169
Mathers, Jerry 18
Matheson, Tim 85, 86, 93, 94, 103, 121, 135, 142
Matthau, Walter 1, 141
Matthews, Kerwin 43
Mattick, Patty 93
Maxwell, Frank 22, 44, 85
McClanahan, Rue 122, 123, 137
McClory, Sean 48
McCord, Joseph 113
McCormick, Nancy 117
McDearmon, David O. 21, 197

McDonough, Kit 161
McEachin, James 85, 99, 116, 117, 125
McGeehan, Pat 9, 12, 13, 15
McGillin, Howard 149, 155
McGinn, James 68, 99, 101, 108, 116, 122, 139, 149, 157, 158, 167, 169, 191
McGivern, William 50, 57, 60, 72, 75, 77, 85, 94, 101, 106, 121, 142, 147, 151, 161, 191
McGowan, Oliver 58
McGreevy, John 1, 126, 127, 131, 135, 139, 141, 144, 151, 156, 158, 162, 191
McGuire, Biff 116, 117
McKeand, Carol Evan 158, 160, 191
McLiam, John 131, 132
McMartin, John 118
McMullan, Jim 104, 116, 117
McMyler, Pam 90, 100, 161
McNally, Steve 18
McVey, Patrick 10, 11
Megna, John 133
Meier, Rupert 38
Menard, Tina 70
Merriweather, Lee 76
Metrano, Art 105, 108
Meyer, Dorothy 121
Michele, Janee (Jannee) 54, 56
Milana, Vincent Duke 79
Miles, Vera 1, 18, 27, 33, 39, 44, 52
Miller, Don 125
Miller, James M. 66, 192
Miller, Marvin 14, 17
Mills, Donna 152
Milner, Martin 58
Missing Person's Bureau 158, 161
Mission of the Apostles, The 8

Mitchell, Don 50, 68
Mitchell, Douglas 71
Mitchell, Particia 155
Mobley, Roger 24
Moessinger, David 26, 47, 63, 75, 90, 99, 104, 108, 192
Mohawk 114, 115
Mohr, Gerald 40
Montalbon, Ricardo 1, 16, 48
Montgomery, Belinda 87, 88
Moody, Ralph 87
Moore, David vii
Moore, Juanita 124
More, Thomas 20
Morgan, Gary 113
Morris, Greg 32, 40
Morris, Howard 58
Morris, Rahsaan 160
Moser, James 1, 9, 33, 41, 49, 60, 63, 70, 106, 112, 141, 142, 143, 144, 146, 147, 148, 159, 192
Moser, Robert 49
Moses, Marian 63
Moss, Ellen 125
Mr. and Mrs. Bliss 151, 152
Mr. Johnson's Had the Course 62, 63
Muldaur, Diana 63, 64, 70, 99
Mulhall, C.S.P., Jack vii
Mullavey, Greg 91, 144, 161, 167, 169
Mummy 61
Mumy, Bill 90
Munson, Donald 56, 59, 192
Murcelo, Karmin 159
Murder in the Family 37, 38
Murphy, Pamela 101
Murray, Jane vii, 167
Myerelink, Victoria
Myers, Pauline 49, 74

Nardini, Tom 89, 104
Navarro, Anna 54
Needle's Eye, The 158, 160
Neely, Jim 157
Nelson, Bek 27
Nesbit, Steve 47
Nettleton, Lois 170, 171, 172
Neuman, E. Jack 9, 192
Newhart, Bob 1, 102, 143
Newland, John 51, 59, 63, 87, 197
Nichols, Nichelle 80
Nitty Gritty Once and Future Now, The 50, 55, 56
No More Mananas 89
No Tears for Kelsey 68
Nobody Loves a Rich Uncle 92, 95
Norman, Maidie 63
North, Edmund H. 1, 92, 95, 192
North, Noelle 149
Norton, Cliff 35
Novello, Jay 17, 24

O'Brien, Carole 30
O'Brien, Edmond 17, 76
O'Connell, Arthur 49, 50
O'Connor, Carroll 39, 70, 71
O'Connor, Glynnis 139
O'Connor, Tim 57, 63, 70, 86
O'Donnell, Penny 22
O'Herlihy, Dan 12, 18
O'Kun, Lan vii, 92, 93, 96, 98, 102, 103, 109, 110, 112, 116, 118, 119, 127, 129, 133, 134, 140, 141, 143, 144, 150, 153, 157, 158, 159, 166, 171, 172, 192
O'Malley, Pat 12, 15
O'Neill, Richard 121, 128
Oates, Warren 148, 149
Ohmart, Ben vii

Old King Cole 75, 80
Oleander Years, The 45
Olfson, Ken 129
Olsen, James 89
One-Armed Man, The 107, 110
Operation Dignity 17
Oppenheimer, Alan 83, 74, 109, 100, 113
Oringer, Barry 47, 101, 192
Orman, Roscoe 140
Out of the Depths 116, 124, 125

Pace, Judy 71, 72
Padilla, Bob 89
Padilla, Jr., Manuel 24
Page, Harry 89
Parfrey, Woodrow 98, 140, 112
Parker, Lara 106
Parrish, Leslie 39
Party, The 90
Pataki, Michael 54, 115, 130, 162
Patrick, Pierre vii
Paul Nickell 44, 197
Paul, St. 187
Paulist Fathers, Paulists vii, 183
Paulist Productions vii, 173, 180
Pendulum, The 126
Penn, William 12
Penny, Don 43
Perennial Problem, The 13
Perez, Jose 159
Perreau, Gigi 58
Perry, Roger 70
Persoff, Nehemiah 82, 106
Petranto, Russ 146, 197
Petrie, Dan 71, 197
Peyser, John 39, 197
Phelps, Tani 79
Phillips, Barney 108, 157

Phony, The 16
Picerni, Paul 14, 15, 22, 23, 77, 85
Picture in Sobel's Window, The 127, 134
Pine, Robert 169
Pinkard, Ron 139
Pius X, Pope 17
Pius XII, Pope 17
Placement Service, The 116, 117, 118
Plumb, Eve 144
Plus Time Served 147, 148
Poker Game, The 68, 69, 70
Politics Can Become a Habit 49
Porous Curtain, The 26
Porter, Don 122
Porter, Peg 112
Post, Ted 1, 30, 31, 36, 47, 170, 174, 197
Prange, Laurie 86, 105, 172
Prather, Joan 107, 121
Prayer from the Abyss 86
Prescott, Guy 11, 12, 17
Pressman, Larry 108, 111, 152
Prince of the Apple Town 68, 69
Prine, Andrew 35, 39, 59, 66, 79, 80
Prisoner, The 21, 22
Proach, Henry 104, 106, 110, 113, 116, 144
Prodigal Father, The 116, 117
Prokash, Joey 124
Prometheus Bound 21, 27, 28
Pryor, Nicholas 174
Purcell, Lee 115, 122, 123, 139

Quigley, Mark vii, xii
Quine, Don 63
Quinn, Bill 98, 112, 113, 157

Rae, Peggy 93
Ragpicker 16

Raines, Beth 133, 137
Rainey, Ford 38, 82, 94, 126, 142
Ralston, Gilbert 1, 33, 36, 192
Ramirez, Frank 89
Ramon, Edgardo 159
Ramsey, Logan 126
Randolph, John 122
Random, Robert 60
Ray, Marguerite 116
Raymond, Gene 12, 17, 69
Reason to Live, A Reason to Die, A 15
Rebirth of Packy Rowe 143
Redd, Mary Robin 110
Redmond, Marge (Marj) 41, 84
Reed, Albert 146
Reed, Marshall 103
Reese, Della 155, 156
Rehearsal 127, 128
Reinhold, Judge 179
Reiser, Robert 99
Renard, David 89
Renard, Ken 72
Rendezvous 163, 164
Resurrection 151, 154
Resurrection of Joe Hammond 105
Reunion 101
Rhodes, Donnelly 61, 106
Rhodes, Mike vii, 136, 137, 138, 139, 140, 141, 142, 143, 144, 146, 147, 148, 149, 150, 151, 152, 153, 155, 156, 157, 158, 159, 160, 161, 162, 163, 165, 166, 167, 168, 169, 170, 171, 172, 174, 176, 177, 198
Rhodes, Robert 89
Rich, John 40, 198
Richards, Paul 31
Richardson, Michael 114
Richman, Mark 27, 57, 79, 80
Ride a Turquois Pony 85, 87, 88
Rifkin, Ron 101
Right-Handed World, The 41
Rist, Robbie 174
Ritter, John 165
Rivas, Carlos 22, 43
Rivas, Carlos 43
Robbie, Seymour 57, 60, 69, 110, 198
Roberts, Clete 12
Roberts, Davis 29, 45
Roberts, Mark 66
Roberts, Michael 125, 130
Robertson, Cliff 185
Robertson, Dennis 95
Robinson, Andrew 142
Robinson, Chris 54
Robinson, John Mark 120, 125
Robinson, Louis 28, 192
Roche, Eugene (Gene) 144, 161, 162
Rodd, Marcia 155, 157
Roley, Sutton 22, 198
Romero 180, 185, 186
Roommates on a Rainy Day 101
Rooney, Wallace 12
Rorke, Haden 77
Rosqui, Tom 130
Ross, Don 36
Ross, Marion 31, 51, 74, 84
Rowe, Misty 106
Ruscio, Al 176

Safren, Dennis 47
Salerno, Charlene 17
Salmi, Albert 33, 40
Sam 68, 73
Sandalmaker, The x, 63
Sandefur, B.W. 35, 192

Sandrich, Jay 138, 141, 143, 144, 150, 165, 174, 198
Santoro, Dean 124
Schaal, Richard 177
Schallert, William 14, 16, 18, 139
Schneider, Stan 79, 89
Scorsese, Martin 151
Scott, Brenda 71
Scott, Bryan 131
Scott, Debralee 116
Scott, Jacqueline 57, 93
Scott, Pippa 48
Scott, Simon 76, 94
Second Chorus 141, 146
Secret Life of God 7
Seed of Dissent 51, 52
Seegar, Sara 34
Senensky, Ralph 1, 57, 69, 71, 75, 79, 80, 96, 112, 120, 124, 136, 147, 148, 157, 167, 168, 198
Serling, Rod 1, 42, 45, 192
Seven Minute Life of James Houseworthy, The 75, 76
Seventeen Forever 122, 123
Seymore, Anne 49, 87, 93
Shalet, Diane 105, 110, 118
Sharma, Barbara 174
Shatner, William 36
She's Waiting for Us 139
Shea, Jack vii, 18, 20, 21, 22, 24, 25, 26, 27, 28, 30, 31, 32, 34, 38, 65, 73, 82, 100, 198
Shea, Michael 90, 107
Shea, Shawn 140
Sheedy, Ally 180
Sheen, Charlie 179
Sheen, Martin 1, 80, 94, 101, 109, 110, 113, 114, 118, 144, 153, 154
Sheldon, James 52, 86, 121, 128, 198
Shelton, Abigail 28
Shepard, Richmond 113
Sherman, Reed 30
Shipman, Nina 28, 39
Shockley, Sallie 85
Siamis, Korby 167, 169, 193
Sierra, Gregory 106, 147, 148, 165
Silva, Henry 22
Simmons, Richard Alan 79, 193
Singh, A.J. 56
Singh, Parki 56
Sinners, Inc 12
Sixth Day, The 158, 159, 160
Slami, Albert 140
Slight Change in Plans, A 147, 149, 183
Slight Drinking Problem, A 135, 137, 138
Sloan, Ron 140
Sloane, Everett 12, 18
Small Statistic, A 54, 55
Smith, Kent 36, 38
Snow in Summer 48
So Little Time 171, 172
Sobieski, Carol 1, 50, 61, 68, 73, 96, 193
Soble, Ron 54
Some Talk About Pool Rooms and Gin Mills 50
Somewhere Before 116, 118, 119
Sommars, Julie 156
Sommerfield, Diane 138
Soodik, Trish 119
Sophomore, The 16
Sorel, Louise 69, 172
Sorensen, Paul 109
Sothern, Ann 28, 74
Soule, Olan 112
Souza, Noel 56
Spanier, Frances 97, 99

Spano, Joe 161
Speilberg, David 165, 166, 171
Spicer, Kyle 172
St. Jacques, Raymond 151
Stacy, James 16, 54, 55
Stalin, Joseph 12, 19
Stanley, Paul 28, 30, 51, 54, 62, 64, 70, 81, 93, 95, 101, 103, 107, 108, 117, 118, 124, 128, 131, 151, 155, 199
Stein, St. Edith 14
Sterling, Tisha 82
Stern, Danny 133
Stevenson, McLean 96
Stich, Patricia 91
Stockwell, Guy 30, 37, 38, 59, 60, 63, 64, 74
Stone, Harold 45
Stone, Leonard 83
Stranger in My Shoes 35, 36
Stratton, Chet 38, 48
Street, Elliot 109, 112
Strickland, Amzie 98, 103, 137
Strong, Michael 110
Strong, Pat 124
Stroud, Don 101, 108, 147, 155
Stuart, Arlen 112
Sugarhill, J.S. 116, 125, 193
Sullivan, Barry 58, 105
Sullivan, Michael vii
Svenson, Bo 146
Sweeney, Terry vii, 108, 113, 114, 116, 124, 133, 136, 137, 138, 139, 140, 141, 159, 160, 161, 162, 163, 165, 166, 167, 168, 169, 170, 171, 172, 174, 176, 177, 193
Sweet, Katie 49
Swenson, Karl 71, 77

Swift, Joan 38
System, The 96, 97

Talbot, Matt 10
Talbot, Nita 105, 152, 174
Tale of Two Testaments, A 6
Tanaka, Dr. 14
Tayback, Victor 115, 119, 120
Taylor, Vaughn 40
Teddy 166
Tedrow, Irene 135
Thea 151, 156
Theft, The 108, 111
Theodore Apstein 42, 188
Thief Named Dismas, I and II, A 33, 41, 42
This Side of Eden 141
Thomas, David 177
Thomas, Daxson 124
Thomas, Ernest 130
Thomas, Marlo 16
Thomas, Philip Michael 138
Thompson, Hilarie 93, 101
Thorton, Phil 15, 199
Thousand Mile Journey, The 33, 34
Thousand Red Flowers, A 71
Three Cornered Flag 59, 62
Throne, Malachi 72, 76
Thunder in Munich 33, 38
Tillich, Paul 43
Tobias, George 103
Tobin, Dan 22
Todd, Thelma x
Tokatyan, Diana Bell 177, 193
Tokatyan, Leon 45, 54, 74, 82, 85, 91, 142, 146, 177, 193
Toomey, Regis 15
Totter, Audrey 82, 83
Townes, Harry 79

Trial by Fire 42, 48
Truck Stop 103
Trujillo, Ron 49, 89
Truth about Time, The 47
Tsu, Irene 63
Tuesday Night Is the Lonliest Night of the Week 69
Turman, Glynn 91
Tuttle, Lurene 85
Tyrants, The 18
Tyson, Cecily 1, 91, 92

UCLA Film and Television Archives xi, xii, 4
Unfinished Business 157, 158
Urchin, The 24

Vacio, Natividad 89
van Dreelan, John 48
van Dyke, Henry 179
Van Patten, Dick 101, 120, 174, 175
Van Patten, Joyce 49, 85, 99
Vegh, Steven 157
Vincent, Keith 13, 14
Vint, Bill 126
Vision of Freedom 11
Vogel, Mitch 115, 139
Volz, Nedra 174
Von Le Fort, Gertrude 10
von Stauffenberg, Claus 18
Vowell, David 122, 193

Walker, Bill 72
Wallace, Marcia 146
Walters, Laurie 136
Walton, Jess 156
War of the Eggs, The 85, 88, 89
Warfield, Maurice 82
Warrick, Ruth 48, 62

Waters, E. Sarsfield (Ed Waters) 21, 31, 39, 47, 54, 60, 64, 67, 75, 84, 90, 107, 193
Watson, Jr., James A. 151
Watts Made Out of Thread 59, 65, 66
We Are the Children 180, 185
Weaver, Lea 72
Webster, Nicholas 89, 90, 199
Weil, Simone 13, 43
Welcome Home 120
Wells, Sheilah 64
Wertz, Hoyt 36
West, Roland x
Westerfield, James 16, 20, 32, 65
What Is a Priest? 9
What Is the Church? 8
What Is the Mass? 9
When Heroes Fall 159
When You See Arcturus 112
Where Are We Going? 8
Where Were You During the Battle of the Bulge, Kid 57
White Star Garage 167, 168
White, Christine 13, 16
White, David 27
White, Peter 168
Whitmore, Stanford 62, 193
Who Has Ever Seen Xanadu 49, 50
Who Is Christ? 7
Whole Damn Human Race, The 57, 58
Why Don't You call Me Skipper Anymore? 94
Why Sparrows Fall 44
Wiggins, Lydia A. 120, 130, 133, 194
Wiles, Gordon 28, 199
Williams, Bill 71
Williams, Cindy 119
Williams, Ike 61

Wilson, Dick 48
Wilson, Flip 144, 145
Wilson, Ty 109
Windom, William 77, 78, 112, 135
Windsor, Marie 79
Wingreen, Jason 56
Winters, Deborah 68, 103
Wintersole, William 82, 169
With a Long Grey Beard 33
Wixted, Michael James 73
Woman of Principle, A 82, 83
Woman Who Changed the World, The 9
Woodpile, The 33, 40
Woodson, William 127
World, Campus, and Sr. Lucy Ann, The 33, 38, 39
Wright, Ben 40
Wrinkle Squad, The 87
Wyatt, Jane 77, 78
Wyenn, Than 57, 84
Wyman, Jane 1, 14, 25, 26, 69
Wynn, Keenan 159, 160

Yancy, Emily 151, 152
Yarnell, Celeste 91
Yniquez, Richard 114, 115
York, Dick 17
Young, Heather 67, 77
Young, John Sacret 1, 167, 172, 173, 194
Yulin, Harris 128

Zadikov, Greg 161
Zimbalist, Jr., Efrem 16, 25, 35, 36, 47, 60, 70, 112, 150, 176
Zodrow, David 85, 87, 194
Zodrow, John 75, 82, 85, 87, 93, 116, 124, 128, 140, 194
Zodrow, Tony 67
Zoller, John 140
Zuchart, William 150
Zwick, Joel 146, 199